B-17
Flying Fortress

MALCOLM V. LOWE

HISTORIC MILITARY AIRCRAFT SERIES, VOLUME 11

Front cover: A natural metal B-17G seen from above, displaying the type's distinctive and well-known shape. The aircraft carries the letter "C" in a square on its starboard outer wing panel, showing assignment to the Eighth Air Force's 96th Bomb Group (BG), based at Snetterton Heath, Norfolk (now the well-known motor racing circuit), from mid-1943 until late 1945. (USAAF/Key Collection)

Title page: B-17G *Mon Tete Rouge II*, 452nd BG, Deopham Green, 1944. (Key Collection)

Contents page: A posed, but nonetheless, informative photograph showing the cramped conditions for the B-17G's two fuselage waist gunners if they were in action at the time. Later B-17G manufacture introduced staggered waist gun positions to relieve this problem. (Malcolm V Lowe Collection)

Published by Key Books
An imprint of Key Publishing Ltd
PO Box 100
Stamford
Lincs PE19 1XQ

www.keypublishing.com

Original edition published as Combat Machines No. 1
*B-17G Flying Fort*ress by Key Publishing Ltd © 2016

ISBN 978 1 80282 313 4

Typeset by SJmagic DESIGN SERVICES, India.

Contents

Introduction

Birth of the legend

The elegant and famous Boeing B-17 Flying Fortress was undoubtedly one of the best-known and most iconic warplanes of World War Two.

It was conceived by the Boeing Aircraft Company (subsidiary to the original Boeing Airplane Company) during the 1930s, principally as a defensive weapon comparable to a flying coastal artillery fortress. It duly became a symbol of the Allied war effort due to the high level of publicity afforded to it during its operational service. Indeed, the B-17 became one of the most important US aircraft of the war, and it played a major part in the Allied bombing campaign against Nazi Germany, which was a decisive factor in the ultimate downfall of the Third Reich in 1945. Eventually, 12,731 B-17s of all versions were built, with initial service test production aircraft being delivered in 1937 and manufacture continuing until 1945, in six major production variants and a host of related models and conversions. The type subsequently also had a long career after World War Two in various different roles for a number of operators around the world.

Historically, the B-17 traces its origins back to the early 1930s. At that time, Boeing was one of the foremost companies exploring the many aviation developments that were gaining acceptance in aerodynamics, streamlining and (for their day) advanced materials. In the 1920s and '30s, Boeing was a much smaller company than nowadays, but nevertheless it was willing to innovate, and produced the beautifully streamlined all-metal Model 200 Monomail single-engined airliner and mail-carrier,

The B-17G was the most numerous production model of the iconic Flying Fortress line. This early "G," 42-31047/MS-T of the 535th BS, 381st BG was named *Wolverine*. It was from the initial G-1-BO production block built by Boeing in Seattle and was shot down on January 30, 1944. (USAAF)

**Eighth Air Force
B-17G-70-BO 43-37704
Button Nose of the 535th
Bomb Squadron (BS),
381st Bomb Group (BG),
Ridgewell. (Key Collection)**

which first flew in May 1930. Subsequently, Boeing created the twin-engined retractable-undercarriage Model 247 airliner, one of the very first modern monoplane multi-engine passenger aircraft. It first flew in February 1933 and placed Boeing in a strong position to gain civil orders. These achievements took place alongside military developments, notably with a twin-engined monoplane bomber, the Boeing B-9 (Model 215/246). Although aerodynamic and advanced for its day, the B-9 design did not gain large orders, partly due to a long-running quarrel between the US Army Air Corps (AAC) and the US Navy over which should operate long-range combat aircraft, and for what reasons. The Navy wanted sole responsibility for American defense with its fleet of aircraft carriers and airships, and it was unwilling to concede ground to the relatively new and ambitious AAC. In the end, the latter was able to achieve the possibility of operating aircraft purely for "coastal defensive" purposes. Within the AAC, there was also an argument between those who advocated a strong fighter arm, and a growing number who supported the idea of strategic bombing via bombers bristling with their own defensive machine guns, which would not need fighter escort due to their own substantial firepower.

Gleaming and looking very advanced for its time, the Boeing 299 is shown during its official roll-out for the press on July 16, 1935. It was the world's first four-engined monoplane bomber with an all-metal structure. (John Batchelor Collection)

AN AEROSPACE GIANT

The Boeing Company (together with its subsidiaries and related businesses) is today one of the few real giants of the aerospace world. It all began with an interest in early aviation technology by entrepreneur William Edward Boeing, a resident of the northwestern US, whose initial aviation company, Pacific Aero Products, was established in 1916. The following year, he set up the Boeing Airplane Company at the start of one of the great industrial success stories of the 20th century. Boeing's commercial products began with the Model C seaplane during World War One, and successfully continued through the often-austere times of the interwar period of the 1920s and '30s. Groundbreaking designs such as the Monomail and 247 airliner showed Boeing's willingness to embrace advances in aviation technology, which placed the company at the forefront of aerospace design and construction. Boeing became one of the chief components of the US "Arsenal of Democracy" during World War Two, which brought the industrial might of the country to bear against the Axis powers. Central to this ascendancy was the B-17 Flying Fortress, a combat-proven success story for Boeing's design and manufacturing prowess. The company survived the run-down in military orders at the end of World War Two relatively successfully, and, in the subsequent decades, Boeing's products became highly successful and world leading. Aircraft such as the iconic 707 and 747 airliners,

and the B-52 Stratofortress bomber, maintained Boeing's leading position as a major aerospace manufacturer. It is a position that the company maintains to this day with such important programs as the 787 Dreamliner civil transport.

Boeing's first major foray into four-engined bomber design was the huge XB-15. With a wingspan of 149ft (45.42m), it was underpowered and just one example was built, but Boeing learned many lessons from this project. (USAAC)

Ambitious requirements

It was against this backdrop of increasing technological advances, crippling financial problems in the US economy, and continuing arguments between and within the American armed services, that the AAC issued ambitious requests for future warplanes in the early 1930s. One of these concentrated on forthcoming bombers, and led to the choice of the twin-engined Martin B-10 monoplane (chosen instead of the Boeing B-9) as the AAC's first "modern" bomber. However, in 1934, a far-reaching official requirement was released. It called for the development of a long-range bomber that could reinforce far-flung outposts of the American empire such as Hawaii, Panama and Alaska or other overseas assets, while also being important for coastal defense in being able to bomb any incoming invasion fleet (in the unlikely event that one would ever appear). This coastal defense role appeased the US Navy sufficiently to enable the requirement to develop into a formal request to the US aviation industry, and one of the companies that responded was Boeing. The result was an enormous four-engined monoplane bomber, the Boeing Model 294 or XBLR-1 (later XB-15), which was a little too ahead of its time, and the available power from existing engines. It finally flew in October 1937, but just one was built. However, the Army also issued a less ambitious requirement in the same year for a future multi-engined bomber, partly as a Martin B-10 replacement. This time, Boeing's designers came up with a workable proposal, which was also ahead of its time. Initially designated the Boeing Model 299, it was intended to be a streamlined four-engined monoplane of all-metal construction. Work commenced on the new aircraft in the summer of 1934, and the prototype was constructed in a very short space of time.

Wearing the civil registration X13372 (an abbreviation of NX13372), the Model 299 was completed in record time considering its size and relative complexity. On July 28, 1935, it made its first flight from Boeing's company airfield at Seattle in the northwestern US, with Boeing test pilot Leslie Tower at the controls. This first aircraft was powered by four 750hp Pratt & Whitney R-1690-E Hornet

An impressive line-up of 2nd Bomb Group (BG) Y1B-17s, showing the strange small nose turret of these very early Fortresses, which was not featured on later versions. When in 2nd BG service, the Y1B-17 designation was sometimes shortened simply to "B-17." (USAAC)

radial engines. Although it was built as a private company venture, the Model 299 still had a military competition to win, and during August it was flown nonstop and at an average speed of 232mph (373km/h) – faster than many contemporary fighters – to Wright Field in Dayton, Ohio, for military testing and evaluation. Sadly, though, disaster struck. The big aircraft's large elevators were normally locked when on the ground to prevent wind damage, the lock being released in the cockpit prior to take-off. On October 30, 1935, the aircraft took off with the lock accidentally still on; it stalled during its take-off climb and plunged to the ground. Two of its crew subsequently died of their injuries, including Leslie Tower. The Model 299 was not at fault, but in the following months, the lion's share of the subsequent bomber contract went to the twin-engined, but much shorter-ranged, Douglas B-18. However, 13 service test Boeings with the designation Y1B-17 were purchased, and B-17 production was up and running. These aircraft were in fact somewhat different to the Model 299 and were called Model 299B. These were, in effect, preproduction aircraft, powered by four Wright GR-1820-39 Cyclone engines of 1,000hp each – all subsequent B-17s were Wright Cyclone–powered. The tragic loss of the Model 299 led to calls for a mandatory checklist for pilots to perform prior to take-off, something that is obligatory in modern flying, but which was not at all commonplace in the 1930s.

The first AAC unit to receive the new Y1B-17 was the 2nd Bombardment Group (Bomb Group or BG) at Langley Field, Virginia, which was fully equipped with the type during the summer of 1937. An additional preproduction airframe, called Y1B-17A, was also built, originally for static test purposes but later to evaluate engine turbo-superchargers (i.e., superchargers driven by recycled engine exhaust gases to enhance power output of its GR-1820-51 engines) for the B-17 to fly at greater and possibly safer heights over its intended targets. During February 1938, six of the small force of 2nd BG Y1B-17s flew a goodwill mission in stages from Langley Field to Buenos Aires in Argentina. By then, the value of the B-17, and of a long-range bomber force, was growing, and production orders eventually materialized for several series-produced models of the B-17. The first of these was the B-17B (Model 299E), the first true production B-17 version; 39 of these were built (first flight June 1939), quite possibly the first turbo-supercharged production aircraft to enter service, which they did in the later summer of 1939. At that time, the B-17B was

Showing the D-shaped vertical tail of early Fortresses, with the code 105 MD, this natural metal B-17C was part of the test fleet of the Material Division at Wright Field, Ohio, where new designs destined for Army Air Corps service were evaluated. (USAAC)

According to this image's official caption, these early USAAC Flying Fortresses were parked at March Field, California; the aircraft in the background has the flat waist gun position of the B-17C and the unit badge of the 88th Observation Squadron. (USAAC)

the fastest and highest-flying bomber in the world and was armed with a variety of handheld machine guns in several positions, including prominent waist blisters. It was followed in 1940 by 38 of the B-17C (Model 299H), with crew armor and flattened waist gun positions, and a prominent "bathtub" fairing beneath the fuselage with two .50 cal machine guns. The first B-17C flew in July 1940, and the B-17D (Model 299H) was a further refinement with improved internal equipment, 42 of which were ordered in 1940.

Combat debut

By this time, World War Two was already in progress. The US was not involved at that stage and was officially neutral, but Britain had already been at war for many months and was in need of modern warplanes. One of the many purchases of American equipment made by the British during that difficult period prior to the instigation of Lend-Lease was a small number of Flying Fortresses. These were B-17C aircraft, 20 being received by Britain (Fortress Mk.I), which were taken from the order of 38 purchased for the US AAC. It is often forgotten that it was Britain's RAF, and not the American services, that first flew the B-17 in combat, this taking place during July 1941. However, the RAF's initial operations revealed a number of technical shortcomings with the basic B-17 layout, especially at high altitude, as well as the need for much more defensive armament.

The early Fortresses, in effect, were not combat-ready, having been designed for defensive rather than offensive purposes, and indeed the B-17D featured a number of alterations in light of the RAF's experiences, including the fitting of self-sealing fuel tanks, increased armament and more armor protection, and cowling gills for better engine cooling. Boeing was, however, already working on improvements to the B-17 design that transformed the aircraft into a very capable warplane indeed.

The B-17F was the most major step on the development line that led to the B-17G, exemplified by 42-30243, a Boeing-built B-17F-95-BO (with external underwing bomb racks) that eventually flew with the 94th BG, Eighth Air Force. (USAAF)

In a major redesign of the layout, Boeing changed the aircraft radically in the next production version, the B-17E (Model 299O), which was the first true combat-ready model. The vertical tail was changed from the "D" shape of the early production versions to the characteristic large, curved structure of the later examples. The horizontal tail was enlarged to give greater area, changing the tailplane span from 33ft 9in (10.29m) of the B-17D to 43ft (13.11m) on the B-17E. These changes all aided control and stability, particularly at high altitude, but the rear fuselage was also altered significantly to allow a tail-gun position to be installed, with two .50 cal machine guns. Two of these weapons were also mounted in a new power turret in the upper fuselage just behind the flight deck, and in a non-retractable ball turret in the lower fuselage. The latter replaced the fixed "bathtub" of the B-17C/D and was originally a remotely controlled turret but was promptly the preserve of the smallest member of the now ten-man crew. More .50 cal guns were also added, handheld, in the radio operator's compartment and in the nose (initially .30 cal guns). In total, 512 B-17Es were ordered, all built by Boeing at Seattle, and the first flew in September 1941. They began entering service in late 1941 with the US Army Air Force(s) (USAAF), which had been created out of the former AAC in June 1941. Of these, 45 were passed to the Royal Air Force (RAF) as the Fortress Mk.IIA. The B-17 was ready for war.

Following the B-17E were two major production versions that were mass-produced, and they subsequently became the backbone of the USAAF's strategic precision daylight bombing campaign against Nazi Germany, and its installations in other parts of occupied Europe. These were the B-17F and B-17G, arguably the two most important Flying Fortress versions and which came to establish the legend of the B-17 in combat. The B-17F (Model 299O/P) was, in effect, an extension of the B-17E but with approximately 400 minor changes, and very important major modifications that were to have an important bearing on the most numerous of the Flying Fortresses, the B-17G (Model 299O/P). These significant alterations to the basic layout, and a full technical breakdown of the B-17G, are described in detail in the following chapter.

The Fortress Mk.IIA was the British equivalent of the B-17E, as shown here by 41-9141 wearing a British-style camouflage finish via American-manufactured paints, although this particular aircraft spent much of its time in the US. (USAAF)

Probably the most famous of all Fortresses was the much-publicized B-17F-10-BO, 41-24485 *Memphis Belle* of the 91st BG's 324th BS, in which, according to popular legend, Captain Robert Morgan and his crew became the first to complete 25 missions in the Eighth Air Force. The crew's 25th trip was nothing like that presented in the titular film directed by Michael Caton-Jones. (USAAF)

Chapter 1

Top of the Range:
Anatomy of the B-17G

Built in larger numbers than any other Flying Fortress model, the B-17G was the ultimate production version of Boeing's famous bomber. It was also the final mark of Flying Fortress constructed, with subsequent derivatives being conversions from baseline "G" manufacture. The B-17G drew on the growing database of knowledge of how the Flying Fortress performed in combat, and it was subject to a number of improvements based on its experience with the enemy, and the requirements of the daylight air war being pursued by the USAAF. To that end, the immediate predecessor of the G, the B-17F, was vitally important. Successive developments with the B-17F, most visibly involving the addition of more defensive firepower, turned the Flying Fortress into just that – a

A classic in-flight image of a B-17G, illustrating several distinctive features of the type including the Bendix chin turret. This particular aircraft, Douglas-built B-17G-30-DL 42-38091, did not enter combat but served stateside with several Base Units (BU) in a secondary role. (USAAF)

true fortress of the air. The operational debut of the RAF Fortress during the summer of 1941, though largely unsuccessful, was vital in highlighting problems with the B-17, and in the wider context this combat baptism showed what would be required in the future for a major daylight bombing campaign against Germany, using high-altitude bombers. The changes made for the B-17E version meant the Flying Fortress had come of age, but subsequent B-17F/G versions were to win universal fame – and no doubt some infamy – in the brutal air war that was waged over Nazi Germany and Occupied Europe later in World War Two.

Continuing evolution

The B-17F, in effect, was an upgraded extension of the B-17E, and featured the very visible adoption of a longer one-piece transparent molded-plastic nose cone (often known by the trade name Plexiglas), as opposed to the shorter and more heavily framed multi-panel transparent nose of the B-17E and earlier versions – which itself had been a radical change from the original, more bulbous stepped nose with a small turret of the Y1B-17. Wider "paddle" propellers were used from the B-17F onwards instead of the narrower blades of the B-17E and earlier versions, causing slight revisions to engine cowling shape, enabling these larger blades to feather (stop, if necessary, in flight) completely. The B-17F also included provision for more fuel, but, in a significant revision to the fuel-carrying capacity of the B-17 series, the existing wing fuel tanks were added to, with additional fuel cells in the outer wing panels (so-called "Tokyo Tanks" – although no one intended that the B-17 would fly missions against the Japanese capital). These gave some 1,110 US gal (4,201 lit) greater usable capacity, increasing the total onboard fuel to approximately 3,630 US gal (13,741 lit), thereby extending the range of this variant considerably.

Just as significant as the extended range of the B-17F, the type also introduced – especially in its later production examples – greater defensive armament. This came in response to the growing amount of

Combat experience proved the need for much greater defensive firepower than was originally installed. *The Bearded Beauty*, B-17F-10-BO LG-O/41-23353 of the 91st BG, had two flexible-mounted forward-firing .50 cal machine guns added, pointing through the Plexiglas nose. (USAAF)

The most obvious feature of all B-17Gs compared to earlier Flying Fortresses was the Bendix chin turret. The extensively glazed Sperry high dome mid-upper turret of later B-17Gs is also visible in this view. (USAAF)

successful fighter attacks B-17s were being subjected to over northwest Europe, during the increasingly heavy US bombing raids on German targets as 1943 wore on. Provision was made for up to three flexible-mounted .50 cal machine guns mounted in the transparent nose cone itself, while the three small side windows in the forward fuselage (ahead of the flight deck on each side) were modified, with one on each side being enlarged to enable a limited forward field of fire for a newly introduced flexible-mounted .50 cal machine gun in a modified mounting. In fact, there were several variations in the layout of these new "cheek" gun windows, some being extended outwards in a special fitting that found its greatest use on the B-17G. External bomb racks were carried under the inner wing section on each side by some B-17F examples, just outboard of the fuselage, to supplement the normal load in the fuselage bomb bay. This proved particularly useful for missions of shorter range.

Production of the B-17F totaled 3,405 examples (2,300 built by Boeing, 605 by Douglas and 500 by Lockheed-Vega). The first B-17F, built by Boeing, flew on May 30, 1942, and the final Boeing-built example was delivered during September 1943. It is also possible that some of the final B-17E production machines were completed to early B-17F standard.

The growing challenge of protecting the Flying Fortress against defending German fighters was also met with a B-17 derivative developed by Boeing, under the designation B-40. This was an up-gunned long-range escort version of the B-17F, intended to "beef-up" the defensive firepower of bomber formations and provide a heavily armed "gunship" escort capable of accompanying the bombers all the way to the target and back. The concept was trialed with an XB-40 (serial number 41-24341), converted by Lockheed-Vega from a standard early B-17F. Several "F"s were eventually finished to this configuration, making 20 YB-40 (some sources say 23 were created; in addition, four of the intended conversions were actually completed as TB-40 trainers). A number of combat trials were carried out over northwest Europe from May 1943, but the heavy and slow YB-40s were not effective. Some of the defensive improvements trialed on the B-40 series were, however, useful in the development of the definitive B-17G layout, including the important innovation of a "chin" turret in the lower forward fuselage.

Extensive manufacture

As with the B-17F, the G was built by all three companies involved in Flying Fortress manufacture – not forgetting the literally hundreds of component suppliers all over the US, subcontracted to provide smaller parts and equipment. In total, 8,680 were constructed – 4,035 by Boeing, 2,395 by Douglas and 2,250 by Lockheed-Vega. The first Boeing-built B-17G flew on May 21, 1943, with the final Seattle-built example being completed in April 1945 – just weeks before the end of the war in Europe. Boeing's production had peaked, according to company figures, with 16 aircraft a day being rolled out during April 1944. The final B-17G, from Lockheed-Vega production, was completed in July 1945. Britain received 98 B-17Gs, redesignated as Fortress Mk.III, mainly for RAF Bomber Command use in specialized electronic warfare and related roles, plus 14 highly modified B-17Fs as the Mk.IIIA.

A late-production B-17F served as a prototype/development testbed for B-17G manufacture, and interestingly many of the initial Gs built were simply add-ons to existing contracts for B-17F construction, again stressing similarities between the two. Indeed, the Boeing Model designation for all later B-17 production remained at Boeing 299O (although some contemporary sources quote the B-17F and G as being Boeing Model 299P).

At the heart of the B-17G's performance was the turbo-supercharger installed for each of the four engines. Externally, part of the turbo-supercharger equipment could be seen beneath each engine nacelle. (John Batchelor Collection)

The Sperry mid-upper turret for the B-17 series had the possibility for different domes to be fitted onto the basic structure. At least six different types of dome have been identified, the example shown here being common to B-17F and some early G usage. (USAAF)

The B-17G was a big warplane. Boeing's own drawings confirm the wingspan as being 103ft 9.38in (31.63m), although many published sources round this down to 103ft 9in. The basic airframe was of all-metal construction, with fabric covering for some of the control surfaces including the rudder. In operational use, the B-17 proved to be very rugged, with a number of well-documented examples successfully struggling back to their bases with extensive damage to their fuselage or wings.

Power for the B-17G came from four Wright R-1820-97 Cyclone nine-cylinder air-cooled single-row radial piston engines, turbo-supercharged, of 1,200hp each. This was basically the same powerplant as the B-17F, but with a higher rating for the turbo-supercharger for greater performance. Each engine was fitted with a General Electric B-2 (later B-22) turbo-supercharger, the US being far ahead of Nazi Germany in this important means of augmenting engine power, with the recycling of engine exhaust gases by the turbo-supercharger.

Although there was theoretically more power available to the B-17G compared to the F, weight increases meant maximum speed was compromised. A lightly laden B-17G could, in theory, reach 302mph (486km/h) at 25,000ft (7,620m), but the accepted maximum speed for a fully laden G at high altitude was just some 287mph (462km/h). This made them considerably slower than the Consolidated B-24 Liberator, alongside which Flying Fortresses went to war over Germany, making mission planning a challenge for Eighth and Fifteenth Air Force personnel.

The most noticeable and significant difference between the B-17F and G was the Bendix remotely operated chin turret. This was an innovation that was derived partly from the unsuccessful YB-40 escort version, but there had already been the intention to introduce some form of chin turret for forward defense against frontal attacks much earlier in B-17 production. It was controlled from inside the nose with a control yoke, had its own reflector sight, and its two .50 cal machine guns were able to elevate 72° and move 172° in azimuth. The introduction of the chin turret brought the G's defensive armament to 13 .50 cal machine guns (two chin turrets, one nose cheek gun each side, two mid-upper Sperry A-1 turrets, two Sperry ball turrets, one in the radio operator's position, one waist gun each side, two tail gun installations).

Above left: Early B-17Gs were a step backwards in being built without the "cheek" gun positions of the B-17F, it being erroneously thought that the new Bendix "chin" turret would provide sufficient forward protection. This is an early Lockheed-built example. (USAAF)

Above right: Being a waist gunner on a B-17F or G prior to the closing-in of these positions in later B-17G manufacture was not a happy profession; the extremely low temperatures coupled with the need to breathe oxygen at high altitude being extremely uncomfortable. (USAAF)

The open waist gun positions of the B-17F were carried over into B-17G manufacture but were eventually refined and enclosed. The tall rectangular device ahead of the gunner's opening was a retractable blast deflector. (USAAF)

The chin turret was in fact not unique to the B-17G and B-40 conversions. As noted previously, there were great similarities between the last production B-17Fs and the first of the Gs, and some late-production F models were actually fitted with the Bendix chin turret. Indeed, two blocks of final B-17F production (the F-80 and F-85-DL of Douglas manufacture) are often called G-1-DL in some listings of B-17 serial numbers.

A further change to the forward end of the B-17G compared to earlier models was a blown Plexiglas clear molding that differed to that of the B-17F, especially in the reduced provision for handheld individual .50 cal machine guns that could be protruded through it. In fact, more than one type of Plexiglas nose cone appeared on B-17Gs, but the firing of the two .50 cal machine guns of the chin

Definitely a B-17F, nonetheless this example from F-120-BO manufacture carries a B-17G cheek gun mount, albeit in the B-17F position of the middle of the three nose-side windows. *Tom Paine* was 42-30793 of the 388th BG. (USAAF)

turret next to the Plexiglas, when pointing upwards near the transparent material, resulted in some cracking. This was cured with blast tubes added to the gun barrels to lessen the effect on the Plexiglas.

Major changes were also made to the cheek gun positions in the forward fuselage of the G compared to the B-17F. Unfortunately, there was a widely held belief that the installation of the Bendix chin turret would make redundant the cheek gun positions in the forward fuselage, which had been introduced on the B-17F. Therefore, some early production B-17Gs actually did away with these and reverted to the three small windows in each side of the nose as seen on the B-17E. This was a mistake, and the cheek gun installations were reinstated, albeit in modified form, in subsequent B-17G production. The starboard machine gun mount was moved one window station rearwards, while the portside mount was placed forward, from the middle of the three side windows (as on the B-17F) to the forward position just behind the Plexiglas nose cone rear edge. This was as a result of the needed stowage space for the chin

Above left: Originally pioneered on the B-17E, the "tail stinger" of the B-17F and early B-17Gs proved effective in providing rearwards defense with its two .50 cal machine guns. (USAAF)

Above right: This badly damaged B-17G-45-DL, presumed to be UX-U/44-6158 of the 92nd BG, illustrated the enclosed waist gun position arrangement of the later production G, and the more extensively glazed high dome Sperry top turret of later B-17G manufacture. (USAAF)

turret's starboard interior-mounted, upward-pivoting control yoke when not in use. These new cheek installations for the B-17G were different to those of the standard fit in the B-17F, having a stepped-out projection for the gun to pivot (rather than the large flush cheek windows of the B-17F), giving a better field of fire. Eventually, a number of B-17Fs – and early B-17Gs not built with them – could also be seen with this installation, presumably through retrofitting "in the field" or at UK modification centers.

Major changes

A further notable progression compared to the B-17F, again brought about by combat experience, was a modification to the waist gun positions of the G. On the B-17F, these were in line, directly across the fuselage from each other, leading to the gunner on either side and often getting in the other's way. Introduced during B-17G manufacture was a staggered waist position to allow the gunners much more room. This was still an open hatch, but in later B-17G production the openings were enclosed, with a modified K-6 gun mount, thus giving hard-pressed gunners much-needed respite from the freezing cold conditions hitherto endured with open hatches.

Seen on later B-17G examples was a complete revision to the tail gun installation. Tail guns had originally been introduced on the B-17E, and the layout as standardized for the B-17F had been continued for B-17G manufacture, in containing its two .50 cal machine guns in a somewhat-pointed rear fuselage with a simple ring-and-bead (post) sight. For later B-17G production, an entirely new installation was adopted. This was fitted to completed B-17Gs at United Air Lines' Cheyenne, Wyoming, modification center, which prepared many B-17Gs for combat operations before delivery to the USAAF for front line use. Sometimes called the "Cheyenne Turret," although it was actually a new mounting rather than a turret, it contained its two handheld .50 cal machine guns within a completely revised rear fuselage structure. The guns had a larger field of fire, and the ring-and-bead site was replaced with an N-8 reflector site. B-17G manufacture introduced this modification in the G-80-BO, G-55-VE, and G-50-DL production blocks. The resulting change to the extreme end of the rear fuselage, together with the addition of the new Plexiglas nose cone, affected the length of the B-17G, with Gs of different rear and front ends being of slightly different lengths.

The standard tail gun position for early production B-17Gs was the same as that for the B-17F shown here, with the two handheld .50 cal machine guns in a relatively long and tapered rear fuselage structure. (USAAF)

A very visible feature of late-production B-17Gs was the so-called "Cheyenne Turret" in the rear fuselage, this revised and roomier gun installation being fitted by United Air Lines' Cheyenne modification center in Wyoming. (USAAF)

The basic crew was ten – pilot, copilot, navigator, bombardier/nose gunner, flight engineer/top turret gunner, radio operator, two waist gunners, ball turret gunner, tail gunner. This number and the crew roles could vary, however. An example was the radar-equipped B-17G PFF Pathfinder lead bombers, which were fitted with a retractable radome in the position normally occupied by the ball turret. This was associated with a version of H2X bombing radar (which itself was derived from the British H2S), and obviously B-17Gs so-equipped did not carry a ball turret gunner; they were sometimes (and subsequently) referred to as "Mickey" (from Mickey Mouse) ships. This radar proved valuable for missions in which the target was obscured by cloud, a frequent occurrence over northwest Europe. Initially, some B-17Fs flew with this radar, the radome on these early examples being mounted beneath the nose; early B-17G conversions also had the radome under the nose, behind the chin turret, before the definitive position in replacement of the ball turret was standardized.

Later in the air war over Europe, with the lessening of Luftwaffe fighter opposition, a number of Flying Fortresses were modified without the chin and ball turrets. This made them look like their predecessor, the B-17F, leading to some confusion as to whether or not they were "friendly" US-operated examples or alternatively clandestine Luftwaffe-flown captured aircraft. On some B-17Gs, the .50 cal machine gun in the radio operator's position in the upper fuselage, ahead of the waist guns position (as introduced on the B-17E), was also removed due to it being deemed of little use later in the war.

Above: **Late in World War Two, a number of B-17Gs had their chin and ball turrets removed, as shown here by S/44-6974 of the 94th BG. (USAAF)**

Right: **The Sperry ball turret of the B-17F and G series went through a number of modifications, but it remained basically the same throughout manufacture. It was not retractable, but it could be jettisoned for belly landings. (USAAF)**

FLYING FORTRESS MANUFACTURING

During World War Two, the US grew into what has often been described as the "Arsenal of Democracy." As soon as they had prepared for wartime production, particularly after the disaster of Pearl Harbor, American factories manufactured prodigious amounts of weapons and all the associated paraphernalia needed to fight a major war. Aircraft construction was undertaken on a huge scale, and this applied as much to the B-17 as any other type. Required numbers for USAAF service meant that, eventually, Flying Fortress manufacture was performed not just by Boeing, but also under contracted license agreements by two of Boeing's usually rival companies – Lockheed and Douglas. All three of these were aviation giants of their time, and all contributed massively to the Allied war effort by their shared manufacture of the B-17F/G.

Both Douglas and Lockheed B-17 production facilities (the latter through its associated Vega division) were located in California, with Boeing manufacture taking place in Seattle. Boeing's original factory site was too small for such extensive construction (except for the earliest examples of Flying Fortress built), and so the company's well-known "Plant Two" (sometimes called "Plant 2" by old Boeing employees) at Seattle undertook much of the B-17 workload. As the war years continued, exponential numbers of women were drawn into the production of warplanes, each one becoming (as was the popular folklore of the time) the famous "Rosie the Riveter," regardless of the actual task. Boeing undertook extensive camouflaging of its Seattle facilities, but it was never subjected to expected or imagined Japanese air raids.

The manufacture of the B-17, as indeed of other military aircraft under USAAF contract, was carried out in specific numbered blocks (batches) within each version. Usually, these blocks of serial numbers were allocated in multiples of five (e.g., B-17G-5-BO, B-17G-10-BO, etc.), but out-of-sequence numbers were sometimes used. A different batch would often introduce detail changes or upgrades compared to the preceding batch, for which there were many during B-17 manufacture. Sometimes, however, just to cloud the picture, a manufacturer would simply introduce a new block number when a fixed number of examples in the preceding block had been completed.

Women workers, the famous "Rosie the Riveter" of wartime propaganda, became increasingly vital in US manufacturing during the years of conflict. Here, several women work inside a B-17 fuselage. (John Batchelor Collection)

B-17 manufacture took place in clean, modern factories well beyond any danger of enemy attack. Here, forward fuselages are being worked on, with part-completed airframes in the distance. (John Batchelor Collection)

SPECIFICATIONS

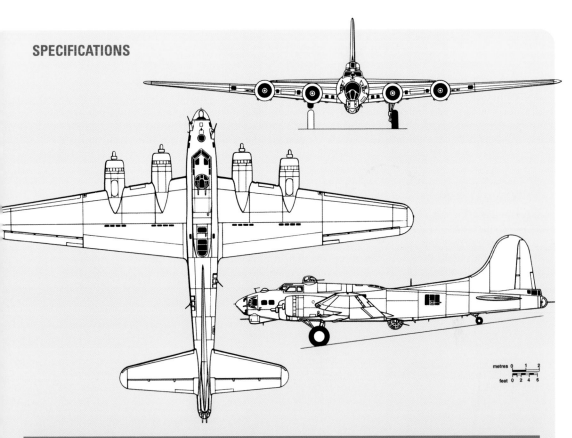

BOEING B-17G FLYING FORTRESS	
Wingspan	103ft 9.38in (31.63m)
Length	74ft 9½in (22.80m) – see note below
Maximum speed	302mph (486km/h) at 25,000ft (7,620m)
Maximum take-off weight	65,500lb (29,710kg)
Range	Approximately 2,000 miles (3,219km) with 4,000lb (1,814kg) bombload
Service ceiling	37,500ft (11,430m)
Armament	11 to 13 (typical) .50 cal machine guns, in various turrets and flexible-mounted; up to some 4,000lb (1,814kg) of bombs for long-range missions
Engine	Four Wright R-1820-97 Cyclone radial piston engines, turbo-supercharged, of 1,200hp each
Crew	Ten

Note: The B-17's well-designed and strong wing layout stayed basically the same throughout production, no matter what version. Many published sources quote the wingspan as being 103ft 9in, but Boeing's own drawings confirm the correct measurement was 103ft 9.38in (31.63m), and that is what is referred to here. The exact length of the B-17G depended on which tail gun installation was carried, the older B-17F-style layout being slightly longer than the United Air Lines "Cheyenne Turret". The two types of clear nose transparency were also of differing dimensions. The length quoted here (74ft 9½in) is taken from Boeing specifications and refers to a B-17G with the older B-17F tail gun installation and larger nose transparency, and includes the gun barrels protruding from the tail.

B-17G SERIAL NUMBERS

B-17 construction efforts during World War Two emerged as one of the great manufacturing feats of the conflict. The three different production locations where B-17s were built (Boeing's plant at Seattle, Washington; Douglas at Long Beach, California; Vega division of Lockheed at Burbank, California) were officially assigned prefix letters to the production blocks of B-17s they built, in addition to the officially assigned serial number of each aircraft they were contracted to build. These were BO for Boeing at Seattle, DL for Douglas at Long Beach, and VE for Lockheed-Vega at Burbank. This applied to B-17F and B-17G manufacture – all early Flying Fortresses up to and including the B-17E were built solely at Seattle. In every instance, the military serial number of each aircraft began with the fiscal year in which the aircraft was ordered. Therefore, for example, B-17G-50-VE/44-8105 was originally procured in the 1944 fiscal year funding. The serial number was usually applied to the vertical tail of the aircraft, but in a slightly abbreviated form, so 44-8105 had "48105" painted across its fin. This particular Flying Fortress flew with the 301st BG of the Fifteenth Air Force as a specially configured PFF Mickey radar-equipped pathfinder, and eventually returned to the US having survived the conflict.

Illustrating the use of serial numbers on B-17s, this belly-landed G-model was officially 44-8483, a later-production G from the G-65-VE production block (i.e., built by Lockheed-Vega). It was coded N8-T of the 600th BS, 398th BG, and eventually flew after repair with the 91st BG.

SERIALS		B-17G-15-DL	42-37804/37893	B-17G-50-VE	44-8101/8200
B-17G-1-BO	42-31032/31131	B-17G-20-DL	42-37894/37988	B-17G-55-VE	44-8201/8300
B-17G-5-BO	42-31132/31231	B-17G-25-DL	42-37989/38083	B-17G-60-VE	44-8301/8400
B-17G-10-BO	42-31232/31331	B-17G-30-DL	42-38084/38213	B-17G-65-VE	44-8401/8500
B-17G-15-BO	42-31332/31431	B-17G-35-DL	42-106984/107233	B-17G-70-VE	44-8501/8600
B-17G-20-BO	42-31432/31631	B-17G-40-DL	44-6001/6125	B-17G-75-VE	44-8601/8700
B-17G-25-BO	42-31632/31731	B-17G-45-DL	44-6126/6250	B-17G-80-VE	44-8701/8800
B-17G-30-BO	42-31732/31931	B-17G-50-DL	44-6251/6500	B-17G-85-VE	44-8801/8900
B-17G-35-BO	42-31932/32116	B-17G-55-DL	44-6501/6625	B-17G-90-VE	44-8901/9000
B-17G-40-BO	42-97058/97172	B-17G-60-DL	44-6626/6750	B-17G-95-VE	44-85492/85591
B-17G-45-BO	42-97173/97407	B-17G-65-DL	44-6751/6875	B-17G-100-VE	44-85592/85691
B-17G-50-BO	42-102379/102543	B-17G-70-DL	44-6876/7000	B-17G-105-VE	44-85692/85791
B-17G-55-BO	42-102544/102743	B-17G-75-DL	44-83236/83360	B-17G-110-VE	44-85792/85841
B-17G-60-BO	42-102744/102978	B-17G-80-DL	44-83361/83485		
B-17G-65-BO	43-37509/37673	B-17G-85-DL	44-83486/83585	PRODUCTION OVERVIEW	
B-17G-70-BO	43-37674/37873	B-17G-90-DL	44-83586/83685	The total of B-17 production by	
B-17G-75-BO	43-37874/38073	B-17G-95-DL	44-83686/83885	version was as follows	
B-17G-80-BO	43-38074/38273	B-17G-1-VE	42-39758/39857	Model 229	1
B-17G-85-BO	43-38274/38473	B-17G-5-VE	42-39858/39957	Y1B-17	13
B-17G-90-BO	43-38474/38673	B-17G-10-VE	42-39958/40057	Y1B-17A	1
B-17G-95-BO	43-38674/38873	B-17G-15-VE	42-97436/97535	B-17B	39
B-17G-100-BO	43-38874/39073	B-16G-20-VE	42-97536/97635	B-17C	38
B-17G-105-BO	43-39074/39273	B-17G-25-VE	42-97636/97735	B-17D	42
B-17G-110-BO	43-39274/39508	B-17G-30-VE	42-97736/97835	B-17E	512
B-17G-5-DL	42-3563	B-17G-35-VE	42-97836/97935	B-17F	3,405
B-17G-10-DL	42-37716	B-17G-40-VE	42-97936/98035	B-17G	8,680
	42-37721/37803	B-17G-45-VE	44-8001/8100	Total manufacture: 12,731 examples	

NOSE ART

Above left: B-17G-40-DL 44-6009/WF-J *Flak Eater*, 364th BS, 305th BG, Chelveston, 1944.

Above right: B-17G *Humpty Dumpty*, 351st BS, 100th BG, Thorpe Abbots, 1944.

Above left: B-17G-90-BO 43-38524 *Blonde Bomber II*, 710th BS, 447th BG, Rattlesden, 1945.

Above right: B-17G *Madam Shoo Shoo*, 551st BS, 385th BG, Great Ashfield, 1944.

Above left: B-17G 42-97061/LL-B *General "Ike"*, 401st BS, 91st BG, Bassingbourn.

Above right: B-17G-100-BO 43-38976/WF-J *She's A Honey*, 305th BG, Chelveston, 1945.

Chapter 2

Eighth Ascendant:
Combat over Northwest Europe

Displaying attributes of early production B-17Gs, including Olive Drab/Neutral Gray paintwork and a lack of cheek guns in the forward fuselage, B-17G-5-BO 42-31134/CC-G, of the 569th BS, 390th BG, was based at Framlingham. It was shot down in September 1944. (USAAF)

The Eighth Army Air Force came into being in February 1944, a fortuitous time for the new organization, because swelling the ranks of its already well-established Bombardment Groups was the latest version of Boeing's famous Flying Fortress, in the form of the B-17G.

Early Eighth Air Force operations

This famous entity has gained its place in popular folklore as the "Mighty Eighth" due to the writings of the famous aviation historian, the late Roger A Freeman. In official terminology, the Eighth Air Force did not exist under that name prior to the events of early 1944, although the term the "Mighty Eighth" has come to refer to the whole time this US strategic air force was based in England. Constituted

originally in the US as VIII Bomber Command on January 19, 1942, it deployed to England during the spring of 1942 with its headquarters at High Wycombe from May 1942 (where it remained until the end of the war in Europe).

The Flying Fortress featured heavily in Eighth operations right from the start; VIII Bomber Command controlled the 97th and 301st BGs, the former being B-17E-equipped. Each was officially designated as a Bombardment Group (Heavy), a term usually abbreviated to Bomb Group or simply BG, with their component squadrons designated and abbreviated in the same way.

Eighth Air Force insignia. (USAAF)

Although this 91st BG B-17F is an example of the austere Flying Fortress layout with which the Eighth Air Force went to war, it has relevance for the later B-17G story, as it was eventually one of several aircraft converted into "flying bombs" for the Aphrodite project and was used against the Mimoyecques underground base of the V-3 long-range gun, which would have been directed against London. (USAAF)

The 97th BG was the first of these two groups to arrive in England and, based at Polebrook, undertook VIII Bomber Command's first-ever raid against targets in Occupied Europe on August 17, 1942, when some of its aircraft bombed rail facilities at Rouen in northern France. The 301st BG arrived a little later with B-17Fs and commenced operations during September 1942. However, just as this small force was starting to make a name for itself, the need for heavy bomber support for the Operation *Torch* invasion of North Africa, and the subsequent fighting there demanded that both groups depart for the Mediterranean Theatre of Operations (MTO) in November 1942. They subsequently served as a part of the Twelfth Air Force and, from November 1943, joined the new Fifteenth Air Force. They both operated B-17Gs later in the war, being among the eventual six heavy bomb groups within the Fifteenth in the MTO.

However, the importance of air operations from England was not diminished with the loss of the two original bomb groups, and eventually the strength of VIII Bomber Command was increased by new groups arriving with their B-17Fs and B-24 Liberators swelling the ranks of the USAAF's daylight bomber offensive. This burgeoned during 1943 and included such infamous raids as those on Schweinfurt and Regensburg (August 17, 1943), which led to heavy losses. It became increasingly

Flying Fortresses were found to need capable, long-range fighter escorts to succeed with daylight precision bombing. Here, a Republic P-47D Thunderbolt, one of the fighter types involved, "beats up" B-17F-75-BO, 42-29930, which flew with the 303rd and 306th BGs, Eighth Air Force. (USAAF)

Above: When the weather was good, and there was a lack of defensive fighters or accurate flak, bombing accuracy could be very good. One of the best examples was this strike on the Focke-Wulf facilities and airfield at Marienburg on October 9, 1943. The bomb pattern at the top of the picture is exceptional. (USAAF)

Left: The introduction of the Bendix chin turret to late B-17F/B-17G manufacture was in direct response to the threat posed from head-on attacks by Luftwaffe fighters, which resulted in so many losses among earlier B-17Fs from late 1942 onwards. This G-model illustrates the classic nose appearance of the sub-type, with the chin turret and cheek handheld .50 cal machine guns. (USAAF)

clear that the cherished doctrine of daylight strategic bombing without fighter escort, embodied in the USAAF since its creation in 1941, was not going to work effectively in the skies over Germany without the input of other elements. Particularly obvious was the need for an escort fighter that could protect the bombers all the way to their targets and back – a fighter with the range of a Flying Fortress. Such an aircraft was not ready in the middle of 1943, although Republic P-47 Thunderbolts of VIII Fighter Command did their best, their endurance extended considerably with the addition of jettisoning long-range fuel tanks beneath their wings.

An important new development took place for VIII Bomber Command during the latter half of 1943, with the appearance of the B-17G during the later months of the year to supplement B-17Fs already in service with several bomb groups. Armed with the chin turret to better defend against frontal fighter attacks, the B-17G was an important addition to the Eighth's available assets. Nevertheless, due to costly daylight raids on increasingly distant targets in Germany, the Eighth needed to regroup. It has been stated by some historians, incorrectly, that the Eighth ceased its bombing raids temporarily. Missions continued without pause, but to less-distant targets where fighter cover was more easily achieved. There was another problem though. The weather over northwest Europe – famously fickle – played havoc with the Eighth's bombing campaign as 1943 ended. Daylight precision raids needed good weather, otherwise the target could not be seen from high altitude, but the number of days when such clear conditions were available grew increasingly rare as the early winter of 1943 drew in. The obvious solution was radar, but this was in its infancy as far as accuracy was concerned. Aircraft carrying ground-mapping radar were sparse in number, and the accuracy was poor; large conurbations could be identified, which was fine for the RAF's night bombing of cities, but for American planners trying to place bombs onto specific factories, it was obviously not of sufficient resolution. Large port cities such as Bremen could be identified by radar due to their proximity to water, and this was another reason why Eighth bombing raids became restricted in scope during the later months of 1943 and the start of 1944 to targets such as this. Nevertheless, sorties the British were carrying out with radar as a bombing aid at that time were making several important breakthroughs, and eventually radar-equipped B-17Gs, using US H2X radar based on British experience with the related (but different) H2S, turned the tide as far as bombing accurately through cloud was concerned.

The Norden bombsight was key to the success of the USAAF's daylight bombing. It enabled the bombardier, through a connection to the B-17's autopilot, to control the bomber over the target, the sight itself releasing the bombs when inputs made by the bombardier coincided. The sight unit is in the upper part of the image, with its mount below. (USAAF)

With its H2X radome extended and bomb doors open, this radar-equipped B-17G, 44-8152 *Miss Ida* from the 457th BG at Glatton, leads the bombing with its own weapons load and smoke marker. (USAAF)

The initial H2X-equipped B-17s arrived in England in early February 1944, and these were first used in combat during February. Initially, some B-17Fs were converted with a strange arrangement whereby the H2X radome was mounted beneath the nose, regardless of whether a chin turret was also installed. Later, however, this ventral hemispherical radome for the radar's rotating dish antenna replaced the ball turret on B-17G Pathfinders, with the electronic black boxes for the Mickey radar set themselves being installed in the radio room just aft of the bomb bay.

The Eighth Air Force came to prize its Mickey ships highly, and they were also used in numbers in the MTO by the Fifteenth Air Force. Those missions where bombing had to be achieved by H2X were

Although this B-17G, 42-97854, was assigned to the 390th BG, the unfortunate aircraft crash-landed in Greenland during its delivery flight across the Atlantic in April 1944. The Fortress is seen here looking rather forlorn in the cold following the crash. (via John Batchelor)

Enclosing the waist windows was one of the most important improvements introduced during B-17G manufacture. Several types of enclosed gun position were adopted, including this heavily framed type with several small windows. (USAAF)

officially documented as "Pathfinder missions," with the aircrew involved being "Pathfinder crews"; this followed the RAF practice of using highly trained Pathfinder aircrew to arrive at the target before the main bomber stream to identify and mark the target with flares. USAAF practice in both Eighth and Fifteenth Air Forces used their Pathfinder crews as lead bombers, with radar-equipped aircraft being followed by formations of standard bombers, which would drop their loads in time with the lead aircraft. All operational B-17Gs were fitted with the famous Norden bombsight, but this would normally be used in each bomber when visual target identification was achievable, otherwise, the H2X method of everyone dropping bombs on the Pathfinder crews' instructions was carried out.

Superlative escort

The real game changer for the US daylight precision-bombing campaign, particularly over northwest Europe, but also in the Mediterranean, was the gradual service introduction of the Packard Merlin-engined North American P-51 Mustang. Originally designed to British requirements but powered by low-level-capable Allison engines, single-seat Mustangs began their service lives with the RAF (in similar fashion to the Flying Fortress), but later served extensively with the USAAF. The installation of the Packard Merlin V-1650 engine turned a low-level fighter and army cooperation aircraft into a high-level fighter of excellent performance. This was in addition to the aircraft's designer and manufacturer, North American Aviation, cleverly building in much provision for internal fuel and the ability of the aircraft to carry jettisoning long-range fuel tanks beneath their wings. At a stroke, this created not just an excellent fighter with good high-level performance, but an aircraft that had great range. Eventually, Mustangs escorted Fortresses and Liberators all the way to distant targets such as Berlin and back with ease.

The importance of the P-51 cannot be overemphasized. Easily capable of looking after itself against Luftwaffe Messerschmitt Bf 109s and Focke-Wulf 190s, it was more than a match for the cumbersome Bf 110s that had hitherto been a major threat to American bombers. Flown by well-trained, highly motivated fighter pilots, Mustangs of the Eighth and Fifteenth Air Forces' fighter groups wreaked havoc among defending Luftwaffe fighters. They even pursued them to their own airfields and strafed those bases when the opportunity arose. The Mustang was truly the war winner in the aerial conflict over Nazi Germany and Occupied Europe. At last, the bombers could be defended from attacking Luftwaffe fighters, even on their longest raids. With the commencement of "Shuttle" missions, whereby Soviet territory in the Ukraine served as distant bases where the Eighth's bombers could stop for rearming and refueling, the bombers were now protected with fighter cover of good quality wherever they flew.

Above: Although apparently suffering damage in this crash-landing, B-17G-85-VE, 44-8844/FC-E of the 571st BS, 390th BG, flew again and was returned to the US at the end of the war. The square on the fin is for the 3rd Air Division of the Eighth Air Force, "J" being the group's code letter. (USAAF)

Left: In the cold, rarefied air above northwest Europe, contrails from the Eighth's bomber formations were a giveaway for the enemy, who would already have picked up the incoming bombers with increasingly sophisticated and capable ground-based radar. This formation of Fortresses would have been visible for miles. (USAAF)

With one exception, all the Eighth Air Force's fighter groups were eventually equipped with the Mustang, in its P-51B, C, D and K versions. The type became similarly important for the Fifteenth Air Force. Merlin Mustangs started to come to the fore at the end of 1943 and in the early months of 1944, just as the B-17G was becoming ascendant. The two types were almost akin to a double-act of capability and strength and held much promise for taking the air war to the Germans in a way that had been impossible before. A Medal of Honor award was made to a Mustang fighter pilot for single-handedly defending 401st BG Flying Fortresses on January 11, 1944. He was James H Howard of the Mustang-equipped 354th Fighter Group (a unit that was part of the Ninth Air Force).

Right: Many B-17Gs featured "pin-ups" on their noses, often painted by talented air or groundcrew. *'Duchess' Daughter* was a B-17G-45-BO, 42-97272/ BN-T of the 359th BS, 303rd BG, based at Molesworth. (USAAF)

Below: *'Duchess' Daughter* came to grief with 30-plus bomb symbols on its forward fuselage to denote sorties flown. (USAAF)

Widespread service

The Eighth Air Force's bombardment elements therefore came to rely very heavily on the B-17G as their principal means of pursuing the strategy of daylight precision bombing against strategic targets in Nazi Germany and occupied Europe. Eventually, no fewer than 27 bomb groups flew the B-17G with the Mighty Eighth, each with four squadrons (a list of these units is included at the end of Chapter 4). These were subdivided for administrative, planning and operational purposes into Bomb Wings (BW), which themselves were a part of the larger Bomb Divisions (BD), later redesignated at the start of 1945 as Air Divisions. Due to its large size, Eighth Air Force contained three Bomb Divisions – of which the 1st and 3rd flew B-17Gs. The 2nd was exclusively a B-24 Liberator organization. The 3rd BD was something of an anomaly in originally having a mix of B-17G and B-24 units, but in the latter half of 1944 its five Liberator groups converted to the B-17G, thus making 3rd BD also an exclusive B-17G entity in addition to the 1st BD. This basic administrative arrangement was somewhat different to the Fifteenth Air Force in Italy, which was a smaller organization and, as described later in this book, just included six B-17G groups, which were administered within its 5th BW.

Take It Easy was a B-17G-75-BO, 43-37895/FC-R of the 571st BS, 390th BG. Assigned to the group in July 1944, it eventually came to grief as seen here during April 1945. Note the Studebaker truck in the background. (USAAF)

BOXING CLEVER

The key elements in the success of the USAAF's daylight bombing campaign over northwest Europe included various factors. The good design of the B-17G itself, the courage of its crews, equipment such as the Norden bombsight, and developing tactics all helped to bring eventual success to the air war that proved so costly in terms of aircrews and aircraft lost in actions.

Developing tactics included the use of a "combat box." This brought together groups of heavy bombers into close formation, to ensure focused firepower against enemy fighters, and enabled a concentration of bombs when the formation dropped together on instructions from its lead bomber(s). Marshalling such a large number of "heavies" into such formations (there would be several boxes on each mission), even though they flew looser until entering the most dangerous moments of each mission, was a major challenge. Some mid-air collisions took place both after take-off and during the bombing phases – it being dangerous to weave and take evasive action while under fighter attack with the bombers flying so closely. The other obvious problem with such tight concentrations was that antiaircraft fire, or "flak," could more easily cause casualties by having a smaller area at which to concentrate fire. Over time, the tactics evolved and the number of bombers in the boxes was reduced, with an intended figure of 27 aircraft usually being employed, thus enabling the bombers more room and making flak bursts less likely to bring down more than one Fortress or Liberator at a time. This resulted in the bomber stream being several miles long; the number of boxes, staggered at different heights, could be high in numbers – particularly if a maximum effort was being staged.

"Pointblank" targets

With the major administrative changes during early 1944, and the growing numbers of B-17Gs and Mustangs coming into service (as well as increased radar technology), the Eighth Air Force was in the best fighting shape it could muster when the weather cleared sufficiently during February 1944, for daylight bombing to be expanded once again to distant German targets.

Discussions that took place firstly at the Casablanca Conference of January 1943, and later at the highly significant Tehran Conference of war leaders (November 28 to December 1, 1943), had a profound effect on war strategy in general, and on the Allied bombing campaign. January 1943 brought the creation of a very significant milestone, called the "Pointblank" Directive, which ordered round-the-clock bombing of German targets, with the RAF bombing at night, and the USAAF by day. At the Casablanca Conference, the Combined Chiefs of Staff agreed to conduct what became known as the Combined Bomber Offensive (CBO), which covered this particular directive. The targets defined by Pointblank were broad in scope: submarine pens, enemy airfields, factories, bridges, rail centers, and anything else that contributed to the ability of Germany to pursue the war.

The Tehran Conference further set out the aims of the "Big Three," and a resultant number of changes took place in the Allied ranks that had a major impact on B-17G crews. A new leadership plan included the naming of General Dwight D Eisenhower to be Supreme Allied Commander for the

There are many images of Fortresses flying through flak-filled skies. This example is typical, a natural metal B-17G, of the 452nd BG, with its bomb doors open. (USAAF)

Although the Fortresses of the Eighth Air Force were intended for strategic bombing missions deep into the heart of the enemy's territory, sometimes they were called on to support ground forces or to aid specific operations. This serene image taken from a B-17G shows just a small part of the D-Day invasion fleet, with the Sandbanks area of Poole, Dorset, in the foreground. (USAAF)

intended D-Day invasion. Similarly, there was a major shuffling of leadership in the USAAF as well, so that General Ira Eaker, who had built the Eighth Air Force and led it through nearly two years of combat, was moved south to become head of the joint USAAF/RAF Mediterranean Allied Air Forces (MAAF). For the head of the USAAF, General "Hap" Arnold, Pointblank and the subsequent discussions at Tehran offered the chance to prove the worth of the US policy of daylight strategic bombing, and the true capabilities of the new B-17Gs and P-51 Mustangs coming to the Eighth Air Force. In this he was to be very successful.

On February 22, 1944, the United States Strategic Air Forces (USSTAF) was established, and with it came the redesignation of the former VIII Bomber Command as (officially) the Eighth Air Force. USSTAF exercised operational control of this reorganized body, as well as having administrative control of the Ninth Air Force in the European Theater of Operations (ETO), and operations of the Twelfth and Fifteenth Air Forces in the MTO. General Carl Spaatz became the commander of this unified organization. During January 1944, James H "Jimmy" Doolittle replaced Eaker to become Commander of the Eighth Air Force, and it was under his leadership that the B-17Gs and P-51 Mustangs subsequently played such a major role in the air war over northwest Europe.

Events did not go particularly well to begin with, however. On January 11, the unpredictable winter weather was good enough to allow England-based bombers to mount a maximum effort. A total of 663 bombers was dispatched to attack aircraft manufacturing facilities at Oschersleben and Halberstadt, on the deepest penetration into the heart of Germany since the major losses of a second Schweinfurt mission on October 14, 1943. As the formation reached the European continent, however, the weather worsened, and the mission was recalled when the leading bombers were just 50 miles (80km) from their targets. Of 238 heavy bombers (including the leading combat wing of the second formation) that continued to their targets, 60 were lost in the subsequent major air battle (including 58 Fortresses). This reflected a disastrous 25 percent loss rate.

Happily, the fortunes of the Eighth Air Force and its ever-growing numbers of B-17Gs improved considerably in the coming months, as recounted later in this book.

Above: B-17Gs of the 613th BS, 401st BG, release their bombs. Smoke markers are just visible in the background. The 401st BG painted its Fortresses with a yellow diagonal tail stripe and letter "S" to denote the group. (USAAF)

Below: There were many uses for B-17Gs. This particular aircraft, G-40-BO 42-97108, was intended for the Royal Air Force (RAF) (as HB771), but it was not delivered and was instead converted into a VIP transport. It is believed to have flown with the Eighth Air Force's Service Command and carried "Invasion Stripes" to deter trigger-happy Allied gunners. (USAAF)

UNCOMMON VALOR

The courage of RAF, Commonwealth and USAAF crews in the combined bombing campaign against Nazi Germany and its allied countries has been well documented. In the case of the Flying Fortress, a number of aircrews who showed particularly meritorious bravery were conferred the highest US military decoration for valor, the Medal of Honor. This decoration is often named incorrectly in published sources as the "Congressional Medal of Honor," which is wrong because it is awarded by the President of the US, who is also commander-in-chief of the US armed forces; it is not awarded directly by the US Congress, only on its behalf by the President.

Many other decorations were awarded to B-17 crew members during the approximately three years the USAAF used the Flying Fortress in combat, and no doubt individual acts of bravery by countless others went unnoticed and unheralded by higher commands. One shining factor that emerges from all the stories of personal acts of heroism by bomber crew members, was the willingness of individuals to work for each other, no matter what the circumstances. Bomber crews in all aircraft types were very much a "family" who had usually trained together – and developed a good working relationship and sense of camaraderie – long before entering combat. Although normally of differing ranks, there is little evidence in the US bomber fraternity of any loftiness on the part of the officers (usually the pilot and copilot, navigator and bombardier) towards enlisted men or NCOs (the remaining crew, including the gunners) aboard the Fortresses.

Pilot Donald J Gott (far left), photographed while training on the B-17 in the US prior to his assignment to the Eighth Air Force's 452nd BG. His posthumous Medal of Honor was gained on November 9, 1944. (USAAF)

Get 'em home

In total, eight B-17G aircrew were awarded the Medal of Honor while serving with the Eighth Air Force, in addition to several others who were flying in B-17Fs or B-24 Liberators. The first three of these B-17G crew members were on the same mission, the famed initial attack of Big Week, February 20, 1944. Flying as a part of the 305th BG contingent at Chelveston, which was briefed to bomb aircraft production plants and related targets in the Leipzig area, 1st Lieutenant William Robert Lawley, Jr., of Leeds, Alabama, was the pilot of new B-17G 42-38109/WF-P of the 364th BS. It had enclosed waist gun positions and a chin turret, but although the latter was intended to ward off head-on attacks by Luftwaffe fighters, the Germans had not got the message at that early stage in the B-17G's combat deployment. The 305th was hit by the frontal attacks of several German fighters as its Fortresses left the target area. Lawley's aircraft was struck in the cockpit by a lethal 20mm round, which killed copilot Lt Paul Murphy and destroyed many of the flight controls. Lawley himself was injured but succeeded in bringing the diving bomber back under control. Several other crew members were also wounded during the air battle in which the 305th found itself. Despite his injuries, and the damaged state of the B-17, and knowing the wounded crew members could not parachute to safety, Lawley elected to fly the long distance from eastern Germany all the way back to Britain. This was duly achieved under the most difficult circumstances, and an emergency landing was successfully made at RAF Redhill. Apart from the dead copilot and one crew member, who parachuted over Germany believing the bomber to be doomed and who became a prisoner of war, all of Lawley's crew survived the mission. Lawley subsequently recovered and, incredibly, flew on several more missions and was awarded the Medal of Honor for saving the lives of his injured crew members.

Sadly, the two further Medals of Honor from February 20, 1944, were both posthumous. Among the B-17Gs that took part in the maximum effort that day by the Eighth Air Force was *Ten Horsepower*, 42-31763/TU-A of the 510th BS, 351st BG based at Polebrook. Akin to Lawley's Fortress, *Ten Horsepower* was struck in the flight deck area by a frontal fighter attack that killed copilot Flight Officer Ronald Bartley and seriously injured the pilot, 2nd Lt Clarence R Nelson, Jr. The bombardier duly exited the stricken bomber by parachute, while three members of ▶

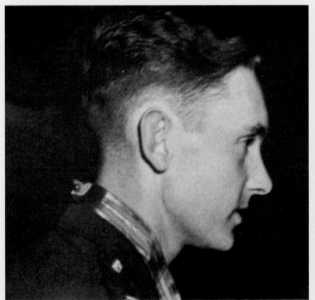 

Above left: B-17G pilot 1st Lieutenant William R Lawley, Jr., of the 305th BG, who was awarded the Medal of Honor for his actions on February 20, 1944. (USAAF)

Above right: Navigator 2nd Lt Walter Truemper was one of the two particularly brave and unselfish airmen aboard the B-17G 42-31763/TU-A *Ten Horsepower*, who died while trying to save the life of their injured pilot on February 20, 1944, the initial raid of Big Week. (USAAF)

Proving that the Medal of Honor is a Presidential (and not a Congressional) award, President Franklin D Roosevelt (seated, left) and Under Secretary of War Robert P Patterson confer the Medal of Honor to Technical Sergeant Forrest L Vosler in the White House on August 31, 1944. A late-model B-17F radio operator/gunner in the 303rd BG, Vosler's actions on the Bremen raid of December 20, 1943, gained him the award for saving his fellow crew members, even though their damaged Fortress had to ditch in the North Sea off Cromer, Norfolk. (National Archives)

Above left: Images of Medal of Honor Fortresses are rare. This belly-landed B-17G-30-DL, 42-38109/WF-P, seen at RAF Redhill, was the aircraft that injured pilot 1st Lt William R Lawley, Jr., of the 364th BS, 305th BG, who flew all the way back to England from eastern Germany, on February 20, 1944. Note the damaged copilot's windows. (USAAF)

Above right: A B-17F crew member awarded the Medal of Honor was Sergeant Maynard H Smith of the 306th BG, for gallantry during his first combat mission on May 1, 1943. He is seen here, in a posed photograph, manning the port waist machine gun in a Flying Fortress. (USAAF)

the crew attempted to bring the badly damaged aircraft under control. Having succeeded in doing this, and despite having no formal pilot training between them, they elected to fly the damaged Fortress all the way back to England in the hope of bringing medical aid to their badly injured pilot. With a considerable feat of airmanship and dodging German defenses they eventually reached Polebrook, where several members of the crew were able to jump safely by parachute. This left Scottish-born engineer/gunner Staff Sergeant Archibald Mathies and the navigator, 2nd Lt Walter Edward Truemper of Aurora, Illinois, attempting to land the damaged Fortress. Although the B-17 was generally a docile aircraft to fly, with relatively easy handling, landing a damaged example was potentially dangerous for even a gifted pilot. Mathies and Truemper had no experience of doing this, and sadly, on their third attempt to land, the bomber crashed and killed the two gallant airmen. Ironically, the wounded pilot survived the crash, but later died of his injuries. Mathies and Truemper were subsequently awarded the Medal of Honor, while two further crew members also received gallantry awards, making the airmen of *Ten Horsepower* the most highly decorated aircrew in the history of the US armed forces.

The price of bravery
Similarly awarded the Medal of Honor while flying in Eighth Air Force B-17Gs were 1st Lt Edward S Michael (305th BG, April 11, 1944), 2nd Lt Robert E Femoyer (447th BG, November 2, 1944), 1st Lt Donald J Gott and 2nd Lt William E Metzger, Jr., (both 452nd BG, November 9, 1944), and Brigadier General Frederick W Castle (of Headquarters, 4th BW, December 24, 1944). All of these awards were posthumous, except for Edward Michael.

In the Fifteenth Air Force, a B-17 crew member was posthumously awarded the Medal of Honor for his actions during one of several raids on a famous oil campaign target – Ploești (modern spelling Ploiești) in Romania. He was 2nd Lt David Richard Kingsley from Portland, Oregon. Kingsley was the bombardier in the crew of pilot 2nd Lt Edwin O Anderson, of the 341st BS, 97th BG. For the June 23, 1944, Ploești mission, Anderson's usual B-17, *Sand Man*, was unavailable, forcing the crew to use one of the 341st's older pool aircraft as a replacement. It was a veteran B-17F, 42-5951 *Opissonya*. Already suffering considerable problems with the aircraft as the raid unfolded, the old B-17 was fatally damaged by flak and fighter attacks during the raid, wounding two gunners. Kingsley successfully gave first aid to both the tail and ball turret gunners, but when the order to bale out was given Kingsley unselfishly gave his parachute to the tail gunner, whose own parachute had been damaged. He then helped the wounded man to exit the aircraft, but duly found himself alone in the stricken B-17 without a parachute of his own. The Flying Fortress subsequently crashed outside the small village of Suhozem in the Plovdiv province of southern Bulgaria. Kingsley's body was found in the

cockpit of the bomber, where he had tried unsuccessfully to execute a crash landing. The remaining nine crew all survived the ordeal, each one being taken prisoner by Bulgarian authorities and later repatriated through Turkey; except for one of the waist gunners, who was picked up by local anti-Nazi partisans, and spent several months in hiding before being returned through Turkey. The crew's subsequent testimony resulted in Kingsley being awarded the Medal of Honor for saving the wounded tail gunner. Tragically, although Kingsley's B-17 had crashed away from the village of Suhozem, it landed among local residents working in the nearby fields, killing seven members of the same family.

The highest-ranking B-17 crew member to be awarded the Medal of Honor was Brigadier General Frederick W Castle, of the Headquarters, 4th Bomb Wing. Castle was in the cockpit of the command B-17G in a major force of US heavy bombers sent to help beleaguered US ground troops on December 24, 1944, during the famous Battle of the Bulge. (USAAF)

Chapter 3

Combat in Warmer Climes:
Early Mediterranean Fortunes

2nd Patches was an often-photographed B-17G of the 99th BG's 346th BS. With the serial number 42-38201, it was a B-17G-30-DL and was assigned originally to the 483rd BG. (USAAF)

Italy's entry into World War Two during June 1940 began a part of that conflict in an entirely new battleground, far away from the momentous events of 1940 in Europe. This new area of operations was the Mediterranean and North Africa, and the conflict there was to have far-reaching implications for the war already being fought in Europe. The B-17G would eventually play a central role in the air war that became an important part of the fighting that raged across North Africa, and eventually on into Italy and then southern Europe.

With British and Commonwealth forces fighting in North Africa to defend the Suez Canal, the US Ninth Air Force was established in April 1942. This was a major statement of intent by the Americans that the defeat of Nazi Germany was a priority for that country's war aims, and it obviously had major implications for the air war in the Mediterranean and North Africa. Henceforward, US tactical and strategic aerial assets would be committed to the region. The Twelfth Air Force was duly established in August 1942, with the famous prewar aviator (but by then a ranking General) Jimmy Doolittle taking command in September. The Twelfth Air Force deployed to England for training and then flew to Algeria to join the Ninth Air Force in support of Operation *Torch*, the Allied landings in North Africa during November 1942. It included B-17 units in its line-up from the start.

Fifteenth Air Force insignia. (USAAF)

A damaged Flying Fortress of the 2nd BG makes an emergency landing at Oudna in Tunisia, shortly before the Fifteenth Air Force moved in its entirety from North Africa to Italy. Some of the Tunisian Fortress bases and landing grounds sat among rugged terrain. (USAAF)

North Africa had been liberated from the Axis powers by the summer of 1943. The final German troops surrendered that May, thus freeing North Africa completely. This had been a ground forces and airpower victory, with the B-17 units in the region playing their part. Allied forces duly crossed the Mediterranean to attack and capture Sicily, starting on July 10, 1943. This was accomplished comparatively easily, despite some pockets of German resistance, again with air power playing an important role. German forces abandoned Sicily in mid-August, and, during September, the prize was in sight. Allied forces at last landed in southern Italy during September. There they began slugging their way north in what became the Naples-Foggia Campaign. Italian dictator Mussolini had already lost power in July, and the new Italian government effectively changed sides later in September, thus freeing to the Allies its air bases in the areas it controlled. Sadly, this did not end the fighting; nearly two years of further action was necessary to defeat Nazi forces that defended positions around Rome

and northward into the Po Valley, an area well protected by the formidable Gustav Line. So, the scene was set for the B-17G to play its part in the air war over southern Europe, in concert with the Eighth Air Force's Fortresses further north.

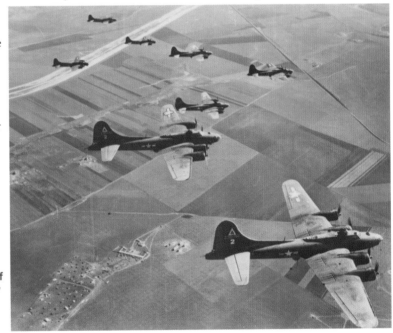

Proving that B-17Fs and Gs often operated together, this mixed formation of both types was from the 97th BG, including examples from the 342nd BS. The performance of the B-17G was not sufficiently dissimilar from the "F" to cause any real operational headaches. (USAAF)

At both Tunisian and later Italian bases of the Fifteenth Air Force, much of the day-to-day maintenance had to be undertaken in the open. This line-up included one of the long-standing B-17Fs that survived well into the B-17G era, probably photographed in March or April 1944. (USAAF)

During the summer and autumn of 1943, the Ninth and Twelfth Air Forces flew in support of ground operations in southern Italy. However, a major reshuffle of US air assets took place during the autumn of 1943. In October, the Ninth Air Force was transferred to England, and was to subsequently play a major role in the ground campaign for occupied France in the anticipated D-Day invasion. It became a tactical air force, losing its bomber assets that had played such an important part in the air campaign in North Africa and Italy up to that time. Its departure led to the birth of the Fifteenth Air Force.

New home for the B-17G
The Fifteenth Air Force was a relative latecomer as a numbered air force in World War Two. Just the Twentieth Air Force, activated during April 1944, and assigned to the Pacific to carry out bombardment of the Japanese home islands, followed the formation of the Fifteenth. The new Fifteenth Air Force, approved during October 1943, was established to meet the growing demand for a purely strategic air force presence to operate over southern Europe, to attack targets not easily reached by the Eighth Air Force and RAF from England.

The creation of the Fifteenth Air Force meant the six veteran heavy bomber groups of the Twelfth Air Force became the nucleus of the USAAF's newest combat air force. What remained of the Twelfth Air Force,

Some missions were flown by Fifteenth Air Force Fortresses at perilously low levels. This was partly due to their support for ground forces, and the often-treacherous terrain that made flying difficult and sometimes hid potential targets. (USAAF)

Marked for several squadrons, this B-17 was with the 301st BG when photographed. The dust indicates dry conditions, which could be as difficult for the Twelfth and Fifteenth "heavies" as the constant rain that was also prevalent. (USAAF)

headquartered at Tunis, Tunisia, was to serve as a tactical air force in support of the northward ground advances in Italy, and later to be involved in the planned invasion of the South of France. The Fifteenth was intended from the start to be a strategic asset, projected to grow to 21 heavy bomber groups (including several with the new B-17G) and seven supporting fighter groups within six months. Their mission was to begin immediate bombing raids against targets in southern Germany and other Axis-supporting countries in southeastern Europe, which were beyond the range of Allied bombers based in England.

The four B-17 groups that formed the core of the Fifteenth Air Force were all combat proven. The Fortress-operating 2nd BG had flown antisubmarine patrols in the Continental US before deploying to the Twelfth Air Force during March to May 1943. The 97th BG was already the most war-proven Bomb Group in Europe. The 97th had deployed to Britain for service with the Eighth based in England during May 1942. It had commenced operations with the B-17E on August 17, 1942, with its initial mission to Rouen in occupied France. The 97th BG transferred to the Twelfth Air Force in November 1942 to support Operation *Torch* and continued to serve in North Africa, Sicily, and Italy until being transferred to the new Fifteenth Air Force during November 1943. The Flying Fortress-equipped 99th BG arrived in North Africa to serve with the Twelfth Air Force, commencing during February 1943, remaining in action until its transfer to the Fifteenth in November. The 301st BG, again a B-17 unit, like the 97th had served firstly with the Eighth in Britain, subsequently deploying to North Africa. There, it served with the Twelfth Air Force, until it too was absorbed by the Fifteenth in November 1943.

Fighter protection was as important over the Mediterranean and southern Europe as it was further north. Here, a B-17G is escorted by a Lockheed P-38J Lightning of the 1st FG, this being one of several fighter units that were also a part of the Fifteenth Air Force. (USAAF)

Antiaircraft fire was a constant hazard to B-17s, either in northern Europe or in the south with the Fifteenth Air Force. This 97th BG formation was photographed braving flak during the bombing of an oil target in Austria. (USAAF)

Two B-24 Liberator Bomb Groups also joined these B-17 units when the Fifteenth Air Force was established on November 1, 1943. As part of the Ninth Air Force, both had participated in the infamous August 1, 1943, low-level raid over Ploeşti, Romania. They were the 98th and 376th BGs.

Command of the new Fifteenth Air Force was delegated to Jimmy Doolittle, who departed the Twelfth Air Force he had built a year earlier for the *Torch* invasion, and which he had led through several bombing missions. He later stated his assignment as the new commander of the Fifteenth was spelled out by his superiors as having four main objectives:

1) To destroy the German air force in the air and on the ground, wherever it might be located within range of our aircraft.
2) To participate in Operation 'Pointblank,' the combined bomber offensive against aircraft plants, ball-bearing manufacturing sites, oil refineries, munitions factories, submarine pens, and airports.
3) To support the ground battle and attack communications facilities on the Italian mainland, along the route through the Brenner Pass, and in Austria.
4) To weaken the German position in the Balkans.

In addition to these goals, targets had to be chosen that would help to pave the way for the intended invasion of southern France. His bombing force would be built around the new B-17G, and the later versions of the B-24 Liberator.

After its establishment on November 1, 1943, the Fifteenth Air Force began flying combat missions while still based in Tunisia. Its Flying Fortress units, which by then were already veterans of considerable combat, were at that time receiving new-build late-model B-17Fs, which were, to all intents and purposes, direct precursors to the B-17Gs that were soon to swell the ranks of these four

Right: The Flying Fortress showed great ruggedness on occasion. B-17G-25-DL 42-38078 *Sweet Pea*, of the 2nd BG's 429th BS, took a direct hit in the fuselage that caused the deaths of three gunners. Nevertheless, the aircraft limped back to safety where it created much curiosity. (USAAF)

Below: Not to be outdone by the enemy, groundcrew successfully rebuilt *Sweet Pea*. The aircraft was made airworthy but apparently did not fly in combat again. (USAAF)

bomb groups, with B-17Gs also being allocated. Some early arrivals of the B-17G found their way to the 97th BG. The lowest numbered G-model from Boeing manufacture that has so far been identified was B-17G-1-BO 42-31044, originally assigned to the Eighth's 100th BG, but transferred to North Africa and the 97th BG's 340th BS, which was still based at Depienne, in Tunisia. This former Luftwaffe airfield was also the home of the 5th BW, which controlled the local heavy bomber groups, firstly under the Twelfth and then the Fifteenth Air Forces, until it transferred to Italy late in 1943.

Italian airfields

Doolittle's orders – and indeed intentions – were to move his new air force as soon as possible to the Italian mainland. The Allied advance up through Italy had released for operational use a growing number of airfields that would be suitable, to one extent or another, for use by heavy bombers. Some of these were in an area to become famous in the annals of Flying Fortress history, the well-known Foggia Plain. From that advanced area of Italy, Doolittle's bombers would be able to effectively overlap the reach of the England-based Eighth Air Force, thus catching Nazi Germany and its allies in a giant airborne pincer. However, these bases were former Axis airfields, some of which were in poor condition having been the target of B-17 and B-24 attention in the preceding weeks. Once the bases around Foggia were rendered operable, the Fifteenth's bombers reached targets in southern France, Germany, Poland, Czechoslovakia, and the Balkans, some of which were difficult to attack from England.

Displaying considerable damage to its vertical tail, B-17G 42-31855 of the 342nd BS, 97th BG, arrives safely at Amendola. The "wound" was inflicted by a Bf 110, but the Fortress was duly repaired and returned to combat. (USAAF)

Major combat operations for the Fifteenth Air Force commenced on November 2, 1943, in a combined B-17/B-24 raid on the Messerschmitt factory, and related production facilities at Wiener Neustadt in northern Austria. From Tunisia, it was a 1,600-mile (2,575km) mission against a facility that had been producing significant numbers of Bf 109 fighters each month. Doolittle's heavy bombers flew through approximately 150 enemy fighters that attacked them amidst, and despite, their own heavy flak. Six Fortresses and five Liberators were shot down, but the accuracy of the bombardment, regardless of flak and fighters, exacted a heavy toll on German aircraft production. According to subsequently examined Austrian documents, production fell from 218 fighters manufactured in October to 80 in November, and just 30 in December.

The Fifteenth Air Force flew missions on 23 days during the month of November, attacking rail lines, submarine pens, bridges, and other targets in Italy, Austria, and Yugoslavia, but, on December 1, 1943, the great day arrived. General Doolittle and his staff moved to Italy with the Fifteenth Air Force headquarters, and duly established themselves at Bari. During December, his fighter and bomber groups gradually moved from Tunisia to Italian airfields. Hastily constructed runways of pierced steel planking (PSP) were laid by US engineers in the Foggia region at several air bases. Those used by the Americans included Amendola, Tortorella, Toretta, Regina, and Cerignola. Fortunately, the weather was reasonably kind in November, but it was not to last. Indeed, in the period 1943–45, Italy was to experience some of the worst weather on record, making life at times unbearable for combat troops and airmen alike.

Worsening weather plagued the Fifteenth Air Force in December. Repeatedly, the entire Fifteenth was grounded because of the weather, and, on marginal days, dispatched bombers found targets obscured by overcast and returned home after dropping their bombs in the sea. It was a frustrating month, not just for Doolittle, but also for the CBO. At the time the Fifteenth was authorized in October, General Hap Arnold and his war planners assumed that weather in the Mediterranean would be more suitable to sustaining air attacks on the Axis by bombers based in Italy, than those in England. In the winter of 1943–44, however, the reverse was true. The B-17G was no less immune to bad weather than the other air assets, and the heavy bombers often remained grounded. The New Year brought better fortunes, although the weather continued to be marginal. The B-17G force, forever growing in numbers, began visiting some of the more exotic locations available to them in Occupied Yugoslavia and the Balkans. In the run-up to Big Week, the famous series of Eighth Air Force raids against vitally important targets in Germany, the Fifteenth's B-17Gs were engaged in support activities from their side of the European continent. At last, German home defenses had to fight on two fronts, meeting incoming bombers in significant numbers from the south as well as from England. This eventually had an increasingly debilitating effect on the German fighter force. Indeed, the fortunes of the B-17G over southern Europe improved dramatically in the final 12 or so months of the war, as described later in this book.

Above: A fighter escort of P-51 Mustangs from the 325th FG "Checkertail Clan" formates on B-17G *2nd Patches*, the much-photographed Flying Fortress of the 99th BG. This fighter unit was also assigned to the Fifteenth Air Force. (USAAF)

Below: Photographed during its bomb run, this B-17G, 44-6325 of the 483rd BG, can be seen almost leaping upwards as its load drops and the aircraft at once becomes lighter. (USAAF)

FORTRESSES IN THE FIFTEENTH

The B-17G made a major contribution to strategic bombing by the Fifteenth Air Force. In total, six groups eventually flew the type under the umbrella of the Fifteenth. These were the 2nd, 97th, 99th, 301st, 463rd, and 483rd. Together, they represented the entire span of Flying Fortress operations in the European theatre. Operationally, they came under the control of the Fifteenth's 5th BW. The 2nd BG had been the pioneer B-17 Group back in 1937 when it received the first service examples of the Y1B-17. It flew the Fortress continuously right to the end of World War Two. The 483rd BG also flew just one type, the B-17, but it was one of the highest-numbered bomb groups formed out of the enormous wartime expansion of combat units within the USAAF. It was activated in September 1943.

Interestingly, the Fifteenth Air Force is more usually remembered as being an organization equipped with the B-24 Liberator. There is some justification for this, because the type was far more numerous than the Fortress during the heyday of strategic bombing in the Mediterranean and southern Europe. Certainly, mission planners in the Fifteenth Air Force had the same general problems as their counterparts in the Eighth, in having to weigh the very different performance envelopes of the two completely dissimilar heavy bomber types.

A 463rd BG radar-equipped "Mickey" Pathfinder, B-17G 44-8247, awaits its next mission. Several of these aircraft in the Fifteenth Air Force appear to have been painted gray overall (possibly Neutral Gray). It also has a yellow rudder. (USAAF)

AIRFIELDS FOR THE B-17G

The giant aircraft carrier

Flying Fortresses needed a considerable amount of infrastructure and large, permanent air bases. These airfields had to be fully equipped with all the necessary amenities, even including their own bomb dumps and fuel facilities. It has rightly been said that, by the height of Eighth Air Force operations, and combined with other Allied air assets, the British Isles had become the equivalent of an enormous aircraft carrier. Each B-17 air base became, in effect, a small town with several thousand men and women working towards the goal of getting a B-17 Group into the air for its next operations. Everything from catering to security had to be handled locally, and in this the Americans usually received friendly (or otherwise) cooperation from their British hosts.

Although a lightly laden Flying Fortress could in theory operate from grass runways, in practice a heavily laden B-17F/G needed a hard and preferably permanent surface. All air bases used by Eighth Air Force Fortresses in

The sight of a bomb group preparing to take off was awe-inspiring and unforgettable. Here, B-17Gs of the 381st BG at Ridgewell taxi out. Air bases had to be large and well-appointed to support the Flying Fortress. (USAAF)

Britain were permanent and of good quality. Some existed before the USAAF arrived, while others were created specially in the early and mid-war years during the extensive period of airfield construction in Britain.

"Permanent" stations such as these had (by the standards of their day) fairly comfortable living quarters and buildings for administration. It was a different story out on the airfields themselves, though, where long-suffering ▶

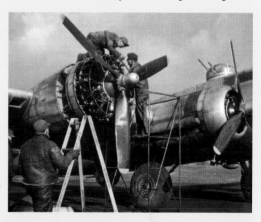

Right: A considerable amount of maintenance and preparation for the next mission had to be carried out in the open, but long-suffering groundcrew of the Eighth and Fifteenth Air Forces performed this with great capability. The starboard outer engine of this natural metal B-17G at Snetterton Heath is worked on by personnel wearing variations of the "Shearling Suit," nowadays often simply called a "bomber jacket." (USAAF)

Below: Major maintenance and preparation of Flying Fortresses for in-theater work was carried out at permanent and well-equipped facilities. Honington was home to the Eighth Air Force's 364th FG, but it also housed the 1st Strategic Air Depot (Troston) and its important work on B-17s, which utilized much of the long-standing airfield's excellent facilities and permanent C-Type hangars, seen here. (USAAF)

Left: Many Eighth Air Force airfields were adjacent to, or indeed built on, existing farmland. With every available piece of land needed in Britain for wartime food production, this "Land Girl" poses while gathering the crops during the summer or early autumn of 1944, in the shadow of B-17G wings. (USAAF)

Below: The airfield at Lucera, in the Foggia area of Italy, was austere and needed repairs before the Fifteenth Air Force could move in. It made a very conspicuous sight from the air. (USAAF)

groundcrew worked in all weathers to maintain the aircraft. Many airfields that hosted bombers had permanent hangars for covered maintenance, but the Fortress was a sizeable machine and most day-to-day work had to be performed out in the open, even if one of their number could be placed inside a hangar. Fortresses that suffered major battle damage would need more extensive work, and this was usually conducted away from the operational airfields, at specialist centers. A considerable amount of small-scale, but nonetheless vital, work was needed on each new arrival B-17F/G to make it combat ready. B-17s were ferried by air to Britain, or to the Mediterranean, and this was the work of Air Depots that catered specifically for individual aircraft types when they arrived in-theater.

The situation in the Mediterranean for the Fortresses of the Fifteenth Air Force, however, was very different to that in Britain. Starting with the North African bases and then on into Italy, facilities varied widely in their overall condition and infrastructure. Most were ex-Axis airfields that were taken by force. Much bomb damage had to be cleared and repaired. Living quarters were often tents, making life for aircrew, maintenance personnel, and all the other staff very difficult at best.

Although the bomber airfields were well behind the front lines, unlike many less permanent landing grounds employed by tactical aircraft, such as those constructed in southern Britain prior to the D-Day landings, this did not make them immune from the enemy. Indeed, on several occasions, Eighth Air Force bombers returning to their British bases from daylight raids were attacked by Luftwaffe intruder aircraft, which produced inevitable casualties.

B-17G CREW ATTIRE

Leather-clad warriors

As with so many aspects of the aerial combat in World War Two, pragmatism and continuing development were of the utmost importance. It became obvious early on that the peacetime crew clothing of the original US AAC would not be good enough for the air war in which the Eighth Air Force was getting more and more deeply involved during 1942–43. This called for considerable improvement of new clothing and paraphernalia – and in some cases the use of existing ideas and equipment from the RAF, which was already combat proven.

Although the B-17G had a theoretical service ceiling of up to approximately 35,000ft (10,668m), this was not attainable in a fully laden state. Normal bombing operations over Germany were usually flown at between 20,000ft (6,096m) and 25,000ft (7,620m). Nevertheless, even at these heights the outside temperature could be around -34 to -50°C (-30 to -58°F). The need for aircrews to be protected from these extremes led to much research, and the gradual introduction of better and more reliable forms of heated clothing. The B-17's cockpit was heated, but the open gunners' stations within the fuselage most certainly were not, and until B-17G production lines introduced enclosed waist windows there was a serious struggle for the gunners to keep warm and operate their weapons effectively.

Aircrews were provided with flight bags so they could carry some of their attire, including body armor, to the aircraft and complete their dressing there. This 379th BG crew trudge wearily back to civilization after their Fortress, B-17G 42-37803 *Carol Dawn*, blew a tire on landing in February 1944. (USAAF)

Briefings for the coming daylight missions were held in the early mornings and could be protracted affairs, with individual crew members such as bombardiers receiving their own specific instructions. Many crew members attended these briefings already partly dressed in their flight clothes, especially in the cold of English and Italian winter days. (USAAF)

Left: Watches were synchronized at the end of a briefing. The carrying of sidearms was not encouraged among the heavy bomber fraternity, although there was apparently leeway depending on Group commanders. The bombardier on the left wears a .45 cal pistol. (USAAF)

Below left: Body armor was vitally important for US bomber crewmen. This Fortress radio operator had a lucky escape when a 20mm round exploded in his radio room, his armored vest literally saving his life. Incidents such as this convinced other crew members to wear the life-protecting armor. (USAAF)

Below right: This posed photograph gives an impression of the cramped and awkward working environment for B-17F/G waist gunners, especially in the days before their gun positions were staggered and enclosed. Oxygen masks could freeze in the open working environment. Once landed, spent cartridge cases were removed by ground personnel. (USAAF)

The staggering and enclosing of the waist gun positions during B-17G manufacture was a significant development, beneficial not just for the two waist gunners, but it also stopped the icy blast from entering the aircraft: hitherto a source of discomfort for the entire crew. Several types of enclosed waist window were introduced during production. These included a heavily framed "barred" type with several small windows within it and a gun mount; a single curved transparent Plexiglas molding with gun mount; and a lesser-seen type with the gun mounting staggered slightly out from the aircraft skin. All these types helped to insulate the B-17G's interior in a way that had not been experienced before, but some gunners found them less suitable for firing their .50 cal machine gun than the previous open position.

The Flying Fortress existed in the days before pressurization for high-flying aircraft was developed into a workable science, and so all members of the crew had to have oxygen available. This was kept in containers within the aircraft but was replenished on the ground after each flight.

Suitable garments

Heavy bomber crews over Occupied Europe were never short of good-quality flying clothing, but much development was needed to achieve the correct combination, and this continued at the end of the war. A typical set of attire for each crew member would start with long woolen underwear, over which would go several layers of insulated and thick attire, some of which could be heated (suitable plug-in points were provided within the B-17's fuselage, run off the type's electrical system). The whole ensemble would be completed with woolen-lined leather flight jackets and trousers. Boots of various types were acceptable, with highly prized RAF flying boots the most sought after. A fleece-lined helmet with earphones was also included – this also went through several phases of development. Perhaps the most iconic piece of attire was the insulated flying jacket. Ultimately, there was a wide range of so-called "bomber jackets," including the sheepskin type most associated with Leslie Irvin, ranging through the A-2 and A-5, with some going under the name of "Shearling Suits" because they were made from the skin of a recently sheared sheep or lamb, which had been tanned and dressed with the wool left on it. These jackets became a part of popular culture following World War Two, and their manufacture in one form or another has continued well after the war ended.

▶

Left: Armored flak vests for bomber crew members were heavy and cumbersome, but these went through their own period of development and refinement. Many airmen only donned them when their aircraft approached a "danger zone." (USAAF)

Below: A 306th BG gunner examines the Sperry top turret of his B-17F. He is well-guarded against the cold, with wool-lined flight jacket and trousers, and suitable insulated flight boots. Turret gunners were better protected from the cold compared to waist gunners, but they found wearing a parachute cumbersome. (USAAF)

Right: A 379th BG crew member wears a classic combination of flight clothing, with the famous but necessary woolen sheepskin-lined leather jacket, sometimes called the "Shearling Suit" or "bomber jacket," as the centerpiece. He carries a steel helmet and chest parachute pack, the harness for which is over his Mae West. (USAAF)

As for parachutes, the Eighth Air Force began operations with a variety of types, some of which were found to be unsuitable. Eventually, bomber crews used a relevant selection of parachutes, which included British chest types. Under the general title of "Observer" parachutes, these were highly successful until developed US-manufactured designs became available during 1944. Pilots normally had a seat pack, gunners a chest or backpack, except for the seated rear gunner with his obligatory backpack. Both Eighth and Fifteenth Air Forces had difficulty in getting some bomber crew members to wear parachutes and body armor, considered by many to be of a restricting nature while trying to perform their tasks within the aircraft. High-profile publicity of crewmen whose lives had been saved wearing the armored vests helped to convince some as to their value, and the installation of flak curtains within the waist gun positions of some later Fortresses went some of the way to helping the always hard-pressed gunners there. Sadly, a number of personnel lost their lives when they could not locate stowed parachutes quickly enough to exit their doomed aircraft.

Above left: One of a sequence of specially made information photographs showing the different flight clothing worn by US heavy bomber crewmen. The airman has almost completed his attire by donning a yellow Mae West inflatable life jacket. He also has a survival knife. (USAAF)

Above right: Although this is a B-24 Liberator crew member, he is representative of all the heavy bomber men (B-24 and B-17 personnel suffered the same deprivations from cold and operations) with his attire, in this case including a B-7 backpack parachute. (USAAF)

Chapter 4

Fortress Dominance:
Triumph over Northwest Europe

The year 1944 did not start in the best way for the England-based bombers of VIII Bomber Command, with the actions of January 11 being particularly difficult. Better weather later in February enabled a return to major operations over Germany.

From February 20 to 25, 1944, USSTAF launched Operation *Argument*, which was a series of specifically targeted missions against Germany that became known as Big Week. The objectives included

Right: A formation of B-17Gs from the 398th BG makes its way towards the target at Neumünster, Germany, on April 13, 1945. By that time in the war over Europe, the B-17G reigned supreme, protected all the way to its targets and back by the equally magnificent P-51 Mustang. (USAAF)

Below: The 91st BG at Bassingbourn was one of the Eighth's premier B-17G units. B-17G-55-DL 44-6578/LG-D of the 322nd BS was named *Rusty Dusty*. (USAAF)

major centers of Germany's aircraft industry, and other key manufacturing sites, but as a byproduct, Doolittle and Spaatz hoped to lure the Luftwaffe into decisive air battles that would allow the Allies greater air superiority in the run-up to the planned cross-Channel invasion during May 1944 (which became D-Day the following month). Big Week was thus vitally important to the Allied war effort and objectives, and playing a central role were the new B-17Gs arriving in increasing numbers from the US for the new Eighth and Fifteenth Air Forces. As a part of the CBO, the RAF was also involved, and began Big Week during the night of February 19–20, by bombing Leipzig. During the day, Eighth Air Force fielded more than 1,000 B-17s and B-24s and 800-plus fighters – one of the biggest raids of the war – in addition to RAF fighters. Around a dozen aircraft factories were attacked, the B-17F/Gs visiting Leipzig to strike at the Allgemeine Transportanlage Gesellschaft Junkers Ju 88 production and Erla Maschinenwerk's Bf 109 Leipzig-Mockau plant, Bernburg-Strenzfeld again for Junkers Ju 88 construction, and the significant AGO facilities at Oschersleben with its Focke-Wulf Fw 190 production. The following day, more than 900 bombers and 700 fighters of the Eighth Air Force struck at more aircraft factories in the Braunschweig (Brunswick) area. On February 24, 1944, the weather cleared over central Germany, and so Eighth Air Force dispatched 800-plus bombers to hit Schweinfurt again and carry out attacks on the Baltic coast. The next day, both Eighth and Fifteenth Air Forces hit numerous targets in southern Germany, including Augsburg and Regensburg, attacking significant Messerschmitt Bf 109 production. Several major air battles ensued during these raids. The Eighth lost 97 B-17s, 40 B-24s, plus others damaged beyond repair; the Fifteenth lost 90 aircraft and US fighter losses were just under 30. The cost to the Luftwaffe was far more, with some factories seriously damaged, hastening the dispersal of important parts of the German aircraft industry – a task never accomplished as competently in Germany as it had been done in Britain earlier in the war. The Luftwaffe's fighter arm (Jagdwaffe) was badly mauled, with several experienced pilots being lost. This was the beginning of the end for the Luftwaffe as a viable fighting force – although it continued to resist right to the end of the war in May 1945, it was rarely again the overall threat that it had been in the preceding years.

The Eighth Air Force was also in a growing position of strength. Lost aircraft could be replenished easily, with the US factories in full uninterrupted production. Well-trained replacement aircrew were also arriving in sufficient numbers to ensure the new B-17Gs were always available. Therefore, just several days after Big Week, Eighth Air Force made its initial significant attack on Berlin – the first major daylight bombing raid on the German capital. On March 6, 1944, more than 700 heavy bombers, along with approximately 800 escorting fighters of the Eighth Air Force, hit numerous targets within Berlin and its environs.

This posed image of a B-17G under repair and receiving new powerplants gives the erroneous impression that it needed at least six engines! The Flying Fortress belonged to the 381st BG, as shown by the letter "L" on its vertical tail. (USAAF)

A contrailing B-17G with its bomb doors open displays its underside details, including much staining aft of the engines plus general wear and tear. (USAAF)

On March 8, 1944, another raid of 600 bombers and 200 fighters bombed the Berlin area again, seriously damaging the VKF ball-bearing plant at Erkner. The next day, H2X radar-equipped B-17Gs led a third attack on Berlin, this time with cloud cover over the capital. In fact, the Eighth Air Force dropped more than 4,800 tons (4,877kg) of high explosive on Berlin during the first week of March.

Known to aircrews as "Big B," Berlin soon became a major target for US bombers. On March 22, more than 800 bombers, again led by H2X radar-equipped pathfinders, hit Berlin yet again, bombing targets though the overcast and causing more destruction to various industries. Because of the thick cloud and rain over the area, the Luftwaffe did not attack the American bomber fleet, as the Germans believed that because of the weather the US assets would be incapable of attacking their targets. However, the pathfinders proved yet again the worth of the B-17G's H2X radar.

Some Flying Fortress nose art was very simple, or just included a name. This is *My Son Bob*, a B-17G-65-BO (43-37514/GD-B) of the 534th BS, 381st BG, based at Ridgewell. (USAAF)

A crash-landed B-17G receives much attention. It was a 379th BG aircraft from the 527th BS, 43-37622/FO-F. The port main undercarriage leg has become detached and lies separately at the right of the picture. (USAAF)

CENTENARIAN B-17Gs

Despite the efficiency of Germany's defenses, both ground-based and in the air, and the protracted nature of the air war over Germany and Occupied Europe, several B-17s succeeded in reaching a creditably high number of individual sorties. Much publicized earlier in the air campaign was the famous B-17F *"Memphis Belle"* of the 91st BG, widely heralded as being the first aircraft and crew to reach 25 sorties (usually named as "missions") – although it was not as straightforward as that. Later in the war, a surprisingly high number of B-17s survived to reach the 100-sorties mark. They included such diverse B-17Gs as *Milk Wagon* and *"E-rat-icator"*, each with its own stories to tell about difficult, and occasionally straightforward trips. In the early days of Eighth Air Force operations, when losses were high, it seemed unlikely that any B-17 or B-24 would be able to reach 100 sorties, but several of these aircraft were lucky and were flown well by their crews (bombers flying on 100 or more missions would certainly see several crews through their tour of duty). There was, however, little sentiment in those war-torn days and, following the end of the conflict in Europe, many B-17Gs were flown back to the US and scrapped. This included centenarians that arguably should have been saved for museum display.

D-Day approaches

The opening of a "Second Front" in the West had been a constant theme in talks between America, Britain and the Soviet Union for a considerable time. Eventually, the planned invasion of France to drive out its German occupiers was scheduled for May 1944. By that phase of the war, it was obvious that such a task would not be easy, and that air power would be needed to play a decisive role in any future operations. With that in mind, air attacks began during February 1944 against many targets across northern France – some in the intended invasion area of Normandy, others further afield to cut supplies in more rear areas and to confuse the enemy as to where the actual landings would take place. Airfields, railway installations, ports and bridges were attacked, as well as known locations of enemy forces. Similarly, airfields used by the Luftwaffe in France and Belgium were hit. Officially, the CBO bombing raids against German fighter production were suspended temporarily on April 1, 1944, and control of Allied aerial assets – including the heavy bombers – passed to General Eisenhower in preparation for the planned invasion.

More than 1,300 Eighth Air Force heavy bombers made an all-out attack on the enemy's rail network on May 1, specifically striking at targets in France and Belgium. On May 7, another 1,000-bomber raid

B-17G-45-DL 44-6163/GD-P was named *Passaic Warrior* and survived the war. It flew with the 534th BS of the 381st BG. (USAAF)

struck additional targets along the English Channel coast, hitting known fortifications, bridges and rail areas; anything that would be of use to the enemy. Attempts were made to minimize civilian casualties where possible during these operations.

During D-Day itself, on June 6, more than 2,300 sorties were flown by Eighth Air Force heavy bombers in the invasion areas and across the wider Normandy area. This was vital, if dangerous, work but it had the effect of concentrating a massive weight of ordnance, aimed specifically at neutralizing enemy coastal defenses and frontline troops, where their locations were known. This "tactical" work was vital to the Allied cause for D-Day to be a success, the weight of the heavy bombers bringing such massive firepower to bear against ground targets being of great value.

Their immediate job accomplished following the D-Day landings, the Eighth's heavy bombers returned to their "normal" work of strategic bombing against much more distant targets, but their firepower remained available should it be needed to help the ground war following the successful D-Day landings.

Large numbers

At the height of these operations during mid-1944, the Eighth Air Force reached a total strength of more than 200,000 personnel, although official estimates claim that more than 350,000 Americans served in the Eighth during the war in Europe. At peak strength, the Eighth fielded 40 heavy bomber and 15 fighter groups, and several specialized support groups. It eventually had the ability to dispatch more than 2,000 heavy bombers and 1,000-plus fighters on a single mission, on a single day, to strike at multiple targets. This was an astounding achievement, and one that has seldom been accomplished during any conflict.

Throughout the rest of 1944, the B-17Gs continued to pound targets in Germany and in other parts of occupied Europe. Cooperation with the Soviet Union was always, at best, insecure, but it did lead to the accomplishment of several Shuttle missions. Otherwise known as Operation *Frantic*, this was a series of seven shuttle-bombing operations conducted by US heavy bombers based either in England (Eighth Air Force) or Italy (Fifteenth) which, instead of returning home after bombing, flew on and landed at three Soviet airfields in the Ukraine. The process began in June 1944 and ended in September. At the Tehran Conference in late November 1943, US President Roosevelt personally proposed the use of Soviet bases by USAAF aircraft to Soviet leader Stalin. A temporary US headquarters detachment at was set up at Poltava airfield, Ukraine, during late April 1944. It was one of three Ukrainian installations operated by the US in that region, the others being Pyriatyn and Myrhorod. They were

Above left: Schnozzle was a B-17G-10-VE, 42-4001 of the 381st BG at Ridgewell. It was lost tragically in a mid-air collision over the home airfield while returning from a raid in January 1945. (USAAF)

Above right: One of the most famous of all Flying Fortresses was *5 Grand*, the 5,000th B-17 built by Boeing, and which was signed by Boeing employees. It went to war with the entire airframe covered in names and was a B-17G-70-BO, 43-37716/BX-H of the 338th BS, 96th BG, at Snetterton Heath.

located along the Kharkov-Kiev railway and were already far behind the front lines. Poltava and Mirgorod were to be used by heavy bombers (both Fortresses and Liberators), while Piriatyn would host long-range escort fighters (Mustangs and P-38 Lightnings). In the event, seven identifiable Shuttle missions were flown under Operation *Frantic*, four by the Eighth Air Force and three by the Fifteenth, between June 2 and September 19, 1944.

In complete contrast, several Flying Fortresses fell into enemy hands during World War Two, and eventually both Germany and Japan had a few flyable B-17s of various marks at their disposal. These aircraft came their way either during military conquest in the case of the Japanese of very early B-17s, or due to downed examples being not too badly damaged and being put back into the air by the Germans. Subsequent German use of captured B-17s is shrouded in folklore and not a little

Many B-17Gs survived to be "repatriated" back to the US where, sadly, most were then scrapped. *Songoon* was a B-17G-65-BO, 43-37565/FC-N of the 571st BS, 390th BG, but is seen here after its return to the US. (USAAF)

over-dramatization. Many stories have circulated as to clandestine employment of these aircraft by the Germans, including plans to bomb high-value targets in England and their ability to infiltrate US bomber formations and take potshots at genuine US-manned bombers. In reality, most airworthy examples were used to familiarize German fighter pilots with the layout and defensive firepower of the B-17, which could be very effective against German fighters if several bombers concentrated their fire in the right direction. Without doubt, however, several German-marked Flying Fortresses did fly with the Luftwaffe's special operations unit KG 200, and it has been claimed widely that the type was given a German designation, "Do 200."

Above: Looking very shiny and new, B-17G-70-DL, 44-6882/ BKJ, flew with the 546th BS of the 384th BG at Grafton Underwood. This is the classic configuration of a late-production Flying Fortress. (USAAF)

Right: A bomber formation, leaving miles of contrails behind the aircraft, was an impressive sight. Unfortunately, these tell-tale emissions would also be good visual reference for the enemy's fighters and ground-based anti-aircraft guns, as seen with this B-17G formation. (USAAF)

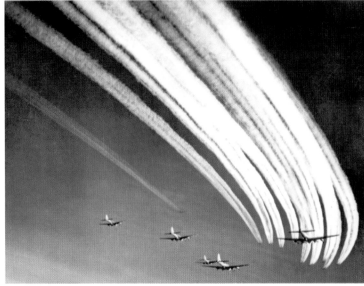

FIGHTER OPPOSITION

The chief opponents of the B-17G in the skies over Nazi Germany and occupied Europe were the single-engined Messerschmitt Bf 109s and Focke-Wulf Fw 190s. Both of these excellent fighters became embroiled in the bitter struggle between the Luftwaffe and the USAAF's daylight bombers over northwest Europe, although neither had been designed specifically to fulfil this role. They were aided by twin-engined Messerschmitt Bf 110 heavy fighters, which again were never originally intended to fight it out high over the Third Reich with heavily armed heavy bombers and their fighter escort. The weapons carried by these types included machine guns, 20mm and 30mm cannon, and unguided aerial rockets. The cannons were particularly deadly against B-17Gs, which, although carrying a certain amount of armor and crew protection, were nonetheless vulnerable to hits from these heavy-caliber weapons. Later in the war, specially armored Fw 190s were trialed, intended to get in close and fight it out with the bombers instead of the quick firing passes employed originally. None, however, were a match for the P-51 Mustang escort fighter which, alongside the P-47 Thunderbolt, easily had the measure of these German types by the latter stages of the air war.

The appearance of the new generation of German fighters late in the conflict potentially threw a lifeline to the Luftwaffe's increasingly overstretched home-defense organization. These were the twin-jet Messerschmitt Me 262 and rocket-powered Messerschmitt Me 163. However, they certainly came under the title of "too little, too late," and the Eighth's fighter pilots soon found ways to combat the Me 262, even though it was a much faster foe. In any case, pilot shortages caused by the number of German fighters being constantly shot down by the US escorts, and the chronic lack of fuel resulting from the highly successful oil/gasoline bombing campaign, plus the destruction of aircraft factories, rendered it impossible for the Luftwaffe to fight on in the skies over Germany as the final days of the war arrived.

Oil targets

The Eighth Air Force was not involved directly in the highly important campaign against Germany's oil/gasoline production centers until May 13, 1944. On that day, 749 bombers, escorted by more than 700 fighters, attacked oil targets in the Leipzig area and at Brüx (modern day Most) in the former Czechoslovakia. After D-Day, in June 1944, attacks on the German oil industry, which was widely dispersed around the Reich, assumed top priority. Large numbers of B-17Gs and Liberators escorted by Mustangs hit refineries and synthetic production plants throughout Germany and the Czech lands during the latter half of 1944 and early 1945. Having almost total air superiority throughout the

Belly-landed *Little Miss Mischief*, a B-17G-35-VE, 42-97880/DF-F of the 324th BS, 91st BG, at Bassingbourn. The aircraft flew 50-plus sorties, and it was apparently repaired after this dramatic arrival. (USAAF)

The damage to the lower forward fuselage of *Little Miss Mischief* was caused by the chin turret when the aircraft was belly-landed. The Fortress was a B-17G-35-VE, 42-97880/DF-F of the 324th BS, 91st BG, stationed at Bassingbourn.

collapsing German Third Reich, the Eighth Air Force could bomb targets as far east as Hungary, while the Fifteenth Air Force hit oil industry facilities in Yugoslavia, Romania, and northeastern Italy. On several occasions, raids were mounted against refineries in Leuna, where most of Germany's synthetic fuel for jet aircraft was being refined. By the end of 1944, Eighth planners concluded that just three out of 91 refineries in Germany or occupied locations were still working normally, 29 were partially functional, and the remainder were destroyed entirely.

Nowadays, guided missiles are commonplace, but in World War Two that sort of technology was in its infancy. Nevertheless, the "black boxes" were being developed in several countries to guide bombs or missiles accurately onto their targets. In the US and Germany in particular, considerable advances were achieved out of wartime necessity, and for the USAAF, this manifested itself in several programs including Aphrodite, which involved B-17s of several marks being converted as actual flying bombs, packed with explosives and radio-guided onto their targets. Several war-weary older B-17Fs and B-17Gs were delegated to be stripped of all armament and usual crew equipment, fitted with radio-control gear, and filled with approximately 20,000lb (9,072kg) of Torpex high explosive. The designation BQ-7 has sometimes been associated with this potentially deadly project. Two crew manned the converted aircraft, set it on course and then baled out while an accompanying B-17 with radio control equipment directed the unmanned explosives-filled B-17 onto its target. Unfortunately, the whole idea was too technically advanced for the radio control equipment of the day and this, plus many other factors, rendered the whole project a complete failure. Several targets were attacked on the European mainland by B-17s operating from England, but with no decent results. After the war, however, some B-17s were converted with radio control equipment as DB-17 drone controllers and QB-17 target drones (Chapter 7 of this book) and used for trials of air-to-air missiles and related testing.

The winter of 1944–45 was yet another inclement season, with military operations hampered by appalling weather conditions. On several occasions, Eighth Air Force bombers returning from

Above: Crash-landed B-17G-50-VE, 44-8151/ CC-O, creates a great deal of local interest in snowy conditions. The Fortress belonged to the 569th BS of the 390th BG – although this crash took place many miles away on the continent. (USAAF)

Left: *Milk Wagon* with its impressive record of individual sorties, denoted by milk bottles. Many, however, were not easy "milk runs." It was a B-17G-70-BO, 43-37756/G of the 708th BS, 447th BG, at Rattlesden.

Some of the "pin-up" artwork could be quite garish. *Puddins Pride* was a B-17G-55-DL, 44-6560 of the 730th BS, 452nd BG, at Deopham Green. (USAAF)

missions had to land wherever possible, with the B-17Gs and Liberators being scattered far and wide. The Germans took advantage of the sometimes-difficult conditions for flying, with the armored thrust that has now become known as the Battle of the Bulge being initially successful, because the Allies were not able to take advantage of their air superiority to support beleaguered ground forces.

On April 7, 1945, the Eighth Air Force put up another maximum effort and dispatched 32 B-17G and B-24 groups and 14 Mustang groups (the sheer numbers of attacking Allied aircraft were so large in 1945, they were officially counted by the group rather than by individual sorties) to targets in the shrinking area of Germany still controlled by the Nazis, hitting the remaining

Above: The 493rd BG at Debach was a B-24 Liberator unit that converted to the B-17G in the latter half of 1944. One of the group's B-17Gs was 43-38190 of the 863rd BS, which survived the war. (USAAF)

Right: A surprisingly high number of B-17Gs flew more than 100 missions, including *"E-rat-icator"*, here being loaded with napalm containers. It was a B-17G-10-V, 42-39970/P of the 730th BS, 452nd BG, from Deopham Green. (USAAF)

airfields where Luftwaffe jets, including the Me 262, were stationed.

The conclusion of the Eighth's successful wartime operations came on April 25, 1945, when the Eighth Air Force dispatched its last maximum effort mission of the European War. B-17Gs hit the Škoda armaments factory at Plzeň (Pilsen), in what is now the Czech Republic, while B-24s bombed rail facilities near to Hitler's mountain retreat at Berchtesgaden. Obviously, the end of World War Two in Europe was a triumph for the Allies, and one of the chief instruments of that hard-fought victory was the B-17G. In concert with the superlative P-51 Mustang, the G had achieved much in the roughly 19 months it had been in combat over northwest Europe. Nevertheless, the ending of the war was in many ways the end for this now-famous warrior. The conflict against Japan in the Pacific was still in progress, and in May 1945 an end to that bloody war seemed a long way off. Already, the B-29 Superfortress was taking over as the USAAF's chief long-range heavy bomber. Flying Fortresses never featured strongly in the Pacific war, where the B-24 Liberator and later the B-29 dominated. There was a plan that some of the operational groups of the Eighth Air Force would re-equip to join the war against Japan, but the Japanese surrender ended this possibility.

EIGHTH AIR FORCE B-17G BOMB GROUPS

Group	Main Airfields in England
34th Bomb Group	Mendlesham
91st Bomb Group	Bassingbourn
92nd Bomb Group	Bovingdon/Alconbury/Podington
94th Bomb Group	Bury St Edmunds
95th Bomb Group	Horham
96th Bomb Group	Snetterton Heath
97th Bomb Group	Grafton Underwood
100th Bomb Group	Thorpe Abbots
303rd Bomb Group	Molesworth
305th Bomb Group	Chelveston
306th Bomb Group	Thurleigh
351st Bomb Group	Polebrook
379th Bomb Group	Kimbolton
381st Bomb Group	Ridgewell
384th Bomb Group	Grafton Underwood
385th Bomb Group	Great Ashfield
388th Bomb Group	Knettishall
390th Bomb Group	Framlingham
398th Bomb Group	Nuthampstead
401st Bomb Group	Deenethorpe
447th bomb Group	Rattlesden
452nd Bomb Group	Deopham Green
457th Bomb Group	Glatton
486th Bomb Group	Sudbury
487th Bomb Group	Lavenham
490th Bomb Group	Eye
493rd Bomb Group	Debach

Eighth Air Force Combat (Bomb) Wing Assignments

1st Combat Wing – 91st, 381st, 398th Bomb Groups

4th Combat Wing – 94th, 447th, 486th, 487th Bomb Groups

40th Combat Wing – 92nd, 305th, 306th Bomb Groups

41st Combat Wing – 303rd, 379th, 384th Bomb Groups

45th Combat Wing – 96th, 388th, 452nd Bomb Groups

93rd Combat Wing – 34th, 385th, 490th, 493rd Bomb Groups

94th Combat Wing – 351st, 401st, 457th Bomb Groups

Assignments at Division Level

1st Bomb Division (later 1st Air Division) Triangle on tail (with Group letter)

91st (A); 92nd (B); 303rd (C); 305th (G); 306th (H); 351st (J); 379th (K); 381st (L); 384th (P); 398th (W); 401st (S); 457th (U).

3rd Bomb Division (later 3rd Air Division) Square on tail (with Group letter)

94th (A); 95th (B); 96th (C); 100th (D); 385th (G); 388th (H); 390th (J); 447th (K); 452nd (L); 486th (W); 487th (P).

EIGHTH AIR FORCE SQUADRON CODES

Code	Sqd/Group							
AW	337/96	H8	835/486	OE	335/95	VP	533/381
BG	334/95	IE	709/447	OR	323/91	WA	524/379
BI	568/390	IJ	710/447	PC	813/482	WF	364/305
BK	546/384	IN	613/401	PU	360/303	WW	369/306
BN	359/303	IR	711/447	PY	407/92	W8	849/490
BO	368/306	IW	614/401	QE	331/94	XA	549/385
BX	338/96	IY	615/401	QJ	339/96	XK	365/305
CC	569/390	JD	545/384	QW	412/95	XM	332/94
CQ	708/447	JJ	422/305	Q4	863/493	XR	349/100
DF	324/91	JW	326/92	Q6	4/34	YB	508/351
DI	570/390	KY	366/305	RD	423/306	2C	838/487
DS	511/351	K8	602/398	RQ	509/351	2G	836/487
EP	351/100	LD	418/100	R2	7/34	2S	834/486
ET	336/95	LF	526/379	R5	839/487	3L	391/34
FC	571/390	LG	322/91	SC	612/401	3O	601/398
FO	527/379	LL	401/91	SG	550/385	3R	832/486
FR	525/379	LN	350/100	SI	814/482	4F	837/487
GD	534/381	MI	812/482	SO	547/384	4N	833/486
GL	410/94	MS	535/381	SU	544/384	6K	730/452
GN	427/303	MZ	413/96	S3	851/490	7D	731/452
GX	548/385	M3	729/452	TS	333/94	7Q	850/490
GY	367/306	NG	860/493	TU	510/351	7W	848/490
G6	861/493	N7	603/398	UX	327/92	8I	18/34
HR	551/385	N8	600/398	VE	532/381	8M	862/493
		NV	325/92	VK	358/303	9Z	728/452

Chapter 5
The Onslaught Continues:
War-Winner over Southern Europe

V
irtually coinciding with the move of the Fifteenth Air Force Headquarters from North Africa to Italy, the famous Tehran Conference of war leaders (Churchill, Roosevelt, and Stalin) was concluding. This would cause American air assets to be altered once more, planning as it did for the final strategy to defeat the Axis in Europe. Roosevelt renewed his 1942 promise to Stalin to open a Western Front, to divide Hitler's ground forces and take pressure off the embattled Russian front. The three nations discussed how best to launch a May 1944 invasion across the English Channel (Operation *Overlord*), as well as invading the South of France (Operation *Dragoon*, originally *Anvil*). Out of those discussions developed a leadership plan including the naming of General Dwight D Eisenhower as Supreme Allied Commander for the D-Day invasion. This move also coincided with a major shuffling of leadership in the USAAF; General Ira Eaker, the popular commander who had built the Eighth Air Force and led it through nearly two years of combat, was moved south to become head of the MAAF, which aimed to coordinate US and RAF aerial assets. General Hap Arnold was also studying the much larger picture of establishing a unified strategic air force in Europe. During January 1944, Jimmy Doolittle had already moved to England to become Commander of the Eighth Air Force, and General Nathan F Twining assumed command of the Fifteenth. It was under Twining's energetic and sometimes excellent leadership that the Fifteenth became the effective southern arm of the US strategic air forces' air war against Germany and its allies. Thus, the B-17G and B-24 Groups of the Fifteenth at once assumed a new importance, with the B-17G in the vanguard of the renewed campaign under Pointblank.

Fifteenth Air Force B-17Gs flew over some of the most spectacular – and potentially deadly – landscapes seen during World War Two. These 97th BG Fortresses negotiate snow-covered mountainous terrain. (USAAF)

With its starboard wing damaged, a 97th BG B-17G flies over a snow-covered town. Flak and enemy fighters were a constant threat for Fifteenth Air Force bombers, in the same way they were for the Eighth Air Force over northwest Europe. (USAAF)

Flying in formation with a combat veteran B-17F, this new natural metal B-17G-55-BO (42-102706) was assigned to the 483rd BG, but it was brought down during a raid in February 1945 by a falling bomb from a B-24 Liberator. (USAAF)

Weather problems

Though the plan had been for these two strategic air forces to strike Germany simultaneously with heavy bombers from two directions, two factors arose in the new year that greatly hampered Fifteenth Air Force operations in fulfilment of the Pointblank Directive. First, poor weather continued to restrict air operations from Italy and indeed over northern Europe. During the days when bombers could take to the air, it became usual to find targets too overcast to bomb. Secondly, on January 22, American forces landed virtually unopposed at Anzio, Italy. While the Germans were unprepared for the Anzio landing, on February 4 they launched a massive assault along the defensive German/Italian Gustav Line that halted virtually all Allied offensives and left American forces at Anzio essentially grounded. This unforeseen situation duly placed heavy demands on the Twelfth Air Force, which had moved from Tunis to Italy in mid-December. To assist, aircraft from the Fifteenth Air Force began regular missions in support of the ground war in Italy.

With no time to enjoy the spectacular Alpine scenery, B-17G 44-6451 of the 419th BS, 301st BG, makes slow progress either to its target or homewards. (USAAF)

The 2nd BG B-17G 42-38078 *Sweet Pea*, which was hit in the fuselage by a flak burst, became a considerable celebrity in Fifteenth Air Force, and was much photographed. (USAAF)

It was not until the last week of February that the weather cleared enough over England and Italy simultaneously for General Spaatz's two air forces to at last prove the validity of their design, with the combined bombing attacks of Big Week. Besides the substantial raids performed by Eighth and Fifteenth Air Force, heavy bombers against many war-related manufacturing centers in Germany, it was also the week in which the Allied air forces began to at last wrest aerial superiority over Europe from the Luftwaffe. It was also a foreshadowing of much more to come in the spring, as new bombers and aircrews arrived in theatre.

A painting of US President Franklin D Roosevelt adorned the nose of *Big Yank* of the 483rd BG. This B-17G, 44-6405, was later converted for search and rescue duties in Italy. (USAAF)

One of the classic images of the Fifteenth Air Force at war included these contrailing B-17Gs of the 97th BG. Above them, their fighter escort of P-38 Lightnings kept watch for enemy fighters. (USAAF)

In Italy, Big Week was followed by six consecutive days of weather so poor that not a single mission could be mounted by the Fifteenth Air Force. Meanwhile, the ground war in and around Anzio continued to be a bitter stalemate as fresh troops and supplies moved in from Germany to reinforce the Gustav Line. To break that stalemate, MAAF launched Operation *Strangle* on March 19. The plan called for both strategic (Fifteenth) and tactical (Twelfth) aircraft to begin interdicting German reinforcement and resupply of the Gustav Line. Almost immediately, US and RAF medium bombers began attacking marshaling yards, rail lines, bridges, and tunnels from Florence to Rome. In support, heavy bombers of the Fifteenth Air Force unloaded tons of bombs on transportation and industrial centers at Turin, Verona, Bologna, and Milan in the German-controlled parts of Italy. Totally in the vanguard of this action were the Flying Fortress units of the Fifteenth Air Force. The number of new B-17Gs had been increasing month by month, enabling many of the older B-17Fs to be retired – although large numbers still soldiered on as air operations intensified.

By March 24, every major supply line to the German front in Italy had been cut and marshaling yards in the north lay in ruins. As a tactical interdiction campaign, Operation *Strangle* was unprecedented in size, scope and duration. On May 11, two months after *Strangle* was implemented, American forces at last broke out at Anzio and began their drive north. The Allies entered and liberated Rome the following month, on June 5, the day before D-Day's Normandy invasion.

On the last day of March, the 463rd BG became operational at Celone, bringing the Fifteenth Air Force to five B-17G heavy bomber groups. It was followed during April by the 483rd BG, stationed initially at Tortorella and then Sterparone. Both groups flew the B-17 exclusively in combat.

With a damaged bomb door and mud-stained lower rear fuselage, this B-17G-50-DL, 44-6430, had been having a bad day. It flew with the 99th BG. (USAAF)

Several B-17Gs of the 97th BG, led by 44-6544 *Kwiturbitchin II* of the 414th BS, fly in a sunlit sky. (USAAF)

Not all B-17s were lost to direct enemy action. 42-102939 seen here while with the 340th BS, 97th BG, suffered a mid-air collision with another B-17G over the Adriatic in March 1945. (USAAF)

The Fifteenth Air Force thus reached its full complement of B-17G groups, numbering six in total. Also incoming were further B-24 Liberator units, swelling the capabilities of the Fifteenth Air Force considerably.

Deadly targets

Improving weather late in March enabled an increased frequency of missions, and on April 2 a 530-bomber attack was flown against the ball-bearing plant and aircraft factory at Steyr, in northern Austria. It was the Fifteenth Air Force's largest formation to date.

Unfortunately, a throng of enemy fighters met the massive formation on April 2 and, despite more than 150 sorties by American fighters in support of the mission, 19 bombers were lost. The following day, 24 heavy bombers went down out of approximately 450 dispatched to bomb targets at Budapest. When 300 B-24s and B-17s returned to Budapest the next day, 13 bombers fell to flak and enemy fighters. With improving weather, the Fifteenth Air Force fielded nearly 2,500 heavy bombers on six consecutive daily raids from April 2 to April 7, but these operations resulted in the loss of some 95 American bombers. Fortunately, in addition to the recently arrived bomb groups brought in to help the Fifteenth achieve its planned strength of 21 heavy bomber groups by May 10, replacement crews were also arriving to fill the gaps in squadrons caused by recent heavy losses.

From then on, the Fifteenth Air Force and its B-17 and B-24 heavy bomber groups were involved in the whole range of Allied air operations. These included striking at many of the objectives intended in the original Pointblank Directive. In addition, missions continued to be flown in support of Allied ground forces, caused by continuing difficulties in making headway against stubborn German resistance. Significant among the strategic directives was the Nazi oil/gasoline industry, and its many associated synthetic production facilities. The Fifteenth Air Force became a frequent visitor to these refineries, which – like the aircraft production plants – were very well defended by anti-aircraft guns and fighters. The Fifteenth Air Force faced not just Luftwaffe aircraft, but also those of Romania and Bulgaria, and the Nazi-supporting Italian forces in the north of Italy. Among the oil targets were the well-known facilities at Ploiești in Romania, and the synthetic oil plants at Blechhammer (known to aircrews as "Black Hammer") in what is now modern-day Poland.

By the spring of 1944, production at Ploiești had increased to some 370,000 metric tons of petroleum products, a commodity critical especially on the Eastern Front. On April 5, 1944, the USAAF at

A radar-equipped Mickey ship of the 483rd BG was followed by several other Fortresses of its unit at Sterparone. It was a B-17G-70-VE, serial number 44-8591. (USAAF)

Right: The airman's name is not known, but the tail is familiar. It belonged to B-17G-35-DL 42-106984 *Glittering Gal*. A combat veteran with the 483rd and 99th BGs, this aircraft was later converted as a staff transport used by 5th Bomb Wing headquarters, wearing on its tail the various geometric device identifiers of the six Fortress-operating bomb groups under its control. (USAAF)

Below: A classic view of B-17Gs over southern Europe. A radar-equipped Mickey B-17G, 44-8105 flies alongside its fellows over typically rugged terrain. It belonged to the 301st BG and had that unit's designators on its fin, and a green rudder. (USAAF)

A well-weathered B-17G of the 2nd BG flies amid flak bursts. It is a Mickey ship with its radome in the position normally occupied by the ball turret. (USAAF)

last returned to Ploiești, with more than 200 Fifteenth Air Force heavy bombers involved. The area's defenses were ready, and 13 bombers were shot down by flak or enemy fighters. Ten days later, more than 400 "heavies" returned, more than half the force attacking Ploiești oil production while the remainder struck at the important marshaling yards at Bucharest. Nine days later, more than 500 heavy bombers repeated the mission.

Ploiești was hit three times in May: on the 5th, 18th, and on the last day of the month. The mission on May 18 illustrates the difficulties from weather and the dangers from enemy aircraft and guns, which plagued nearly all missions into that infamous target. More than 400 heavy bombers were dispatched, including 35 Flying Fortresses from the 463rd BG. The latter was later awarded a Distinguished Unit Citation for its actions that day, one of several such accolades to the B-17G groups of the Fifteenth.

As well as the oil/gasoline targets, there were other missions, such as those to the deadly Weiner-Neustadt Messerschmitt factories, which cost more than 40 bombers downed in two missions in May alone. Ploiești was the target again on June 6 when more than 500 "heavies" attacked the oil refineries.

"Shuttle" missions

In a bid to aid the West's major ally in the East, the Soviet Union, in June 1944, the Fifteenth Air Force bombed railway networks in southeast Europe, in support of Soviet military operations in Romania. Throughout the summer of 1944, the Austrian aircraft manufacturing centers at Wiener Neustadt were bombed, and oil-producing assets continued to be attacked. On June 2, the Fifteenth Air Force flew its first Shuttle mission when some 130 B-17s and P-51 escorts landed in Russian-controlled territory after a raid against Hungarian targets. Two more such Shuttle missions followed.

During July 1944, the Fifteenth began attacking targets in southern France in preparation for Operation *Dragoon*, the Allied invasion of the South of France. Several important French towns

In The Bag, a B-17G either being worked on or salvaged. Its barely discernible data plate behind the kangaroo suggests it is either 44-6264 or 44-6764; both served with the 2nd BG at Amendola, the former was hit by an RAF aircraft in a parking accident. (USAAF)

Officially this 463rd BG B-17G 44-6686 crashed on operations during March 1945, but mysteriously it also appears to have been operated by Soviet forces. In this view, what appears to be a Russian officer stands near the aircraft. (via John Batchelor)

and cities, including Toulon (with its port and naval facilities), Marseilles, Lyon, and Grenoble, were bombed by the Fifteenth's B-17s and B-24s, with attempts made as far as possible to minimize civilian casualties. Subsequent operations aided Allied ground forces following the landings themselves on August 15, 1944.

The winter of 1944–45 was particularly harsh, again compromising what could be achieved with strategic bombers, and it was not until the spring of 1945 that operations quickened again. A famous Fifteenth Air Force mission was staged on March 24, 1945, when 666 bombers struck Berlin, Munich, and other German targets, as well as centers in the former Czechoslovakia. The Berlin force was attacked by Me 262 jets that inflicted losses (ten bombers and five fighters) while the defending Mustangs claimed eight jets downed. With, at last, the winding down of the air war, the final major effort came on April 25, when 467 bombers struck rail targets in Austria,

Fifteenth Army Air Force – B-17G Bomb Groups	
Bomb Group	Assigned Bomb Squadrons
2nd BG	20th, 49th, 96th, 429th BS
97th BG	340th, 341st, 342nd, 414th, BS
99th BG	346th, 347th, 348th, 416th BS
301st BG	32nd, 352nd, 353rd, 419th BS
463rd BG	772nd, 773rd, 774th, 775th BS
483rd BG	815th, 816th, 817th, 840th BS
All six Bomb Groups were subordinate within Fifteenth Air Force to the 5th Bombardment Wing.	

Italian airfields used by Fifteenth Air Force B-17G units	
Amendola	(2nd BG, 97th BG)
Celone	(463rd BG)
Cerignola	(97th BG, 301st BG)
Foggia	(2nd BG briefly)
Lucera	(301st BG)
Marcianise	(97th BG briefly, 99th BG briefly)
Pisa	(483rd briefly)
Sterparone	(483rd BG)
Tortorella	(99th BG, 483rd BG)
Note: the brief tenures of some groups at particular locations were usually at the end of the war, or just after when the group was either being deactivated or rotated back to the US.	

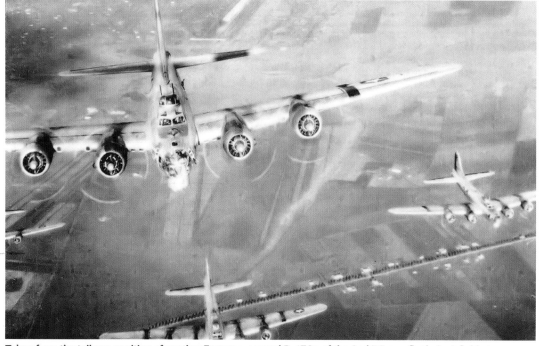

Taken from the tail gun position of another Fortress, several B-17Gs of the 2nd BG overfly their airfield at Amendola, in the Foggia area of Italy, during early morning sunlight. (USAAF)

severing communications into Czechoslovakia. The Fifteenth's final bombing mission was flown on May 1, 1944, when B-17s attacked Salzburg rail targets in Austria. With the German surrender in Italy, the Fifteenth's heavy bombers began dropping supplies particularly over Yugoslavia. The evacuation of then-freed Allied prisoners of war was also undertaken.

At its peak, during the latter half of 1944, the Fifteenth Air Force numbered approximately 1,200 heavy bombers operational at any given time. Its aircraft had ranged far and wide over southern Europe and the Balkans and had contributed to the final Allied triumph in May 1945. The war against the Nazi oil/gasoline industry was crucial, in concert with similar coordinated operations of the Eighth Air Force. The Fifteenth Air Force was inactivated in Italy on September 15, 1945. There had been a plan echoing that of the Eighth Air Force's, that some operational groups would re-equip to join the war against Japan, but following Japanese surrender, that did not happen.

A fine air-to-air photograph of Douglas-built B-17G-50-DL 44-6379 operated by the 96th BS of the 2nd BG, Fifteenth Air Force. (Malcolm V Lowe Collection)

Chapter 6
British Missions:
RAF Operations

Long before the dramatic exploits of the USAAF's B-17G fleet had taken place, the first B-17s flown in combat were the early C models (Fortress Mk.I) of the RAF's 90 Squadron, Bomber Command, during July 1941. Some historians state the lack of success achieved in these early operations as the reason why the B-17 never served in large numbers with the RAF. Whatever the reason, the RAF received just a comparatively small total of B-17s of various versions.

Twenty Fortress Mk.Is were followed by the Mk.IIA (B-17E equivalent) and the Mk.II (B-17F), both of which served with squadrons of Coastal Command where their exceptional endurance proved important on long-range anti-submarine patrols. One of the principal operators was 220 Squadron, which had flown Fortresses since receiving ex-90 Squadron Fortress Mk.Is during late 1941 and early 1942.

The B-17G was supplied initially to Britain during 1944 as the Fortress Mk.III, but this involved just 98 aircraft from Boeing and Lockheed-Vega production. Their serial numbers were HB761-HB820, KH998-KH999, KJ100-KJ127 and KL830-KL837. Of these, however, approximately 13 were repossessed for US service and were apparently not delivered for frontline RAF operations (some being assigned to the Eighth Air Force's 388th BG) – which explains why some published sources state that

Images of 100 Group Fortress Mk.IIIs in flight are rare. KH999/BU-W served with 214 Squadron, based at RAF Oulton. (Malcolm V Lowe Collection)

With its forward fuselage (cheek) windows over-painted and a prominent "flame-damper" visible beneath its outboard engine, Fortress Mk.III HB796 has the tall Type 313 transmission mast amidships, and smaller spine aerial for the Airborne Cigar jammer. It later served with 214 Squadron. (Malcolm V Lowe Collection)

the RAF actually received 85 Mk.III aircraft. In British service, the B-17 of any version was usually referred to (including in official documents) simply as a "Fortress" and not a "Flying Fortress," and an Mk.III is often referred to as a B.III.

Clandestine war

Although Bomber Command had no use for the Fortress as a standard night bomber following the early war experiences with Fortress Mk.Is, the B-17G nevertheless was to play a vital role in the RAF's night bombing offensive against Nazi Germany. This involved some Mk.IIIs being converted for Radio Counter Measures (RCM) work, later called Electronic Counter Measures (ECM), to fly with the RAF's specialist 100 Group. Their role was to combat German defenses, particularly radar, to protect the RAF's main force of Lancaster and Halifax bombers. The Fortresses intended for this task were seconded to Scottish Aviation Ltd at Prestwick for conversion. Most were fitted with a prominent radome under the forward fuselage for H2S radar equipment, replacing the standard Bendix chin turret of the B-17G. H2S was used as a ground-mapping radar by the RAF as an aid to night area bombing, and was also fitted to Main Force Lancaster and Halifax bombers. There were many other alterations made to the Fortresses, including the installation of various jamming equipment. Indeed, it appears that no two aircraft were the same in their equipment fits. In addition, the RAF also received 14 specially converted B-17Fs directly from Eighth Air Force stocks for ECM work (additional to the aforementioned Mk.II/B-17F airframes), which are sometimes called Fortress Mk.IIIA (serials SR376–SR389). The Eighth Air Force was additionally involved in this form of clandestine and highly secret electronic warfare, and there was considerable collaboration between the RAF and USAAF on this task.

Two 100 Group squadrons flew the Fortress Mk.III on electronic warfare operations. The first of these, 214 (Federated Malay States) Squadron (code letters BU), was based at RAF Oulton from May 1944. Its Fortresses were joined by those of 223 Squadron (code 6G), a Consolidated Liberator unit at Oulton, late in the war; the latter unit flew its first RCM Fortress sorties in April 1945. The Fortress Mk.IIIs of these two squadrons flew in support of Main Force bomber operations with RCM, as well as "Window" (chaff-dropping), support. A Fortress training unit, 1969 Flight, was also stationed at Oulton.

A 100 Group Fortress Mk.III apparently put "out to pasture" at the end of the war. It had a rare, semi-clear radome beneath its forward fuselage for British H2S radar equipment. (Malcolm V Lowe Collection)

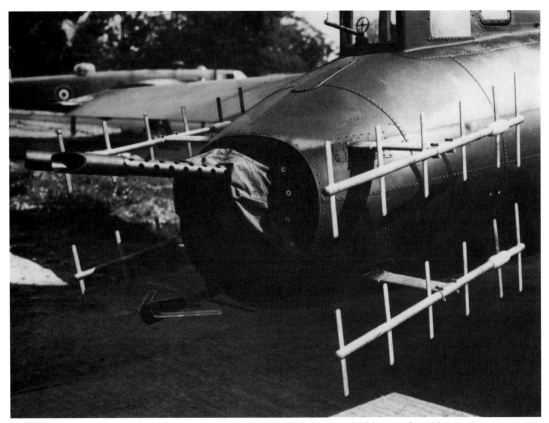

The "tail stinger" of a 100 Group Fortress Mk.III; the TV-like aerials on each side were for Airborne Grocer equipment, aimed to jam German airborne interception radars. The smaller lower antenna was a Monica IIIE tail warning radar transmission aerial, its receivers being two diminutive blades on each side of the fin. (John Batchelor Collection)

Involvement in the clandestine RCM war was no guarantee of safety for the Fortresses, however, and several were shot down by German defenses. A particularly costly occasion was the night of March 14–15, 1945. Bomber Command's targets that night included oil facilities in the Lützkendorf area, as part of the significant oil/gasoline bombing campaign. 214 Squadron provided jamming support, but its aircraft appear to have become detached from the Main Force bombers, enabling Luftwaffe night fighters to make several successful attacks. It was also costly for 214 Squadron itself and two of its Fortress Mk.IIIs, HB802 and HB799 (one published source claims HB779). Both were attacked by aircraft of NJG 6, the two Fortresses probably successfully fired upon by the radio/radar operator of the Junkers Ju 88G-6 night fighter coded 2Z+MF of Hauptmann Martin Becker, Kommandeur of IV./NJG 6. Crew members of HB802 baled out before the Fortress crashed, but the pilot of HB799 managed to bring his crippled Fortress in for a crash-landing at Bassingbourn after the remaining nine crew members baled out over German-held territory.

The conclusion of World War Two in Europe was the end of the road for many of 100 Group's special Fortresses, and a number were put out to pasture at 51 Maintenance Unit, RAF Lichfield (Fradley). Most of the RAF's Fortresses (except for the Mk.I examples) were supplied under Lend-Lease arrangements with the Americans, who did not require their return, so many were simply scrapped. However, some examples did soldier on into the early postwar era and the commencement of the Cold War. The need for ECM work did not stop with the end of World War Two, and several Fortress Mk.IIIs served with the Radio Warfare Establishment at RAF Watton in the months following the end of the war.

FORTRESS B. MK.III
CYCLONE
AUGUST 1944

The RAF used the B-17G (Fortress Mk.III) for RCM duties with squadrons of 100 Group during 1944–45. This Mk.III with black-painted undersides has the prominent fairing under the forward fuselage for British H2S radar. A Consolidated Liberator is visible to the right. (John Batchelor Collection)

Left: Many RAF 100 Group Fortress Mk.IIIs carried a large radome for British H2S radar equipment beneath the forward fuselage, where the B-17G's chin turret was usually installed. Conversion work was carried out by Scottish Aviation Ltd at Prestwick. (John Batchelor Collection)

Below: A 100 Group Fortress Mk.III displays its trademark rear antennas. These aircraft often, but not always, carried a nine-man crew and were festooned with aerials for the secret "black boxes" fitted within the fuselage. (Malcolm V Lowe Collection)

Maritime operations

The B-17G also served with the RAF's Coastal Command, albeit again in comparatively small numbers (code ZZ), which had flown Fortresses of various marks since receiving ex-90 Squadron Fortress Mk.Is during late 1941 and early 1942. According to the latest available research, Coastal Command Fortresses were involved in the sinking of 11 U-boats, either wholly or in conjunction with other Allied aircraft or ships. Five of these involved 220 Squadron aircraft, with 206 Squadron also featuring prominently – these "kills" were achieved with earlier marks of Fortresses. 220 Squadron was based at Lagens in the Azores from the autumn of 1943 for long-range patrol work, and these aircraft helped alongside British-operated Liberators to close the "Atlantic Gap," in which German U-boats had operated beyond the range of previous maritime patrol aircraft. In addition to its existing Fortresses, the squadron eventually received a small number of Fortress Mk.IIIs from the summer of 1944 onwards, an example being HB791 (ex-42-98021), which was coded ZZ-T.

A further squadron that used late-model Fortresses, during 1945, was 251 Squadron (code AD), based at Keflavík airfield near Reykjavík in Iceland. Again, this squadron was a long-standing operator of Fortresses of various types and was engaged primarily in meteorological reconnaissance. It was in the latter role that Fortresses continued in Coastal Command service after the end of World War Two (251 Squadron was disbanded during October 1945), with several examples being Struck Off Charge as late as 1947, when the remaining Fortresses appear to have ended their association with the RAF.

Images of Fortress Mk.IIIs in Coastal Command service are rare. Believed to have been photographed in the Azores while with 220 Squadron, HB791/ZZ-T (ex-42-98021) was fitted with a ventral radome for sea search-configured H2S radar. (John Batchelor Collection)

Chapter 7

Postwar Performance

B y the end of World War Two in the Pacific, Boeing's B-29 Superfortress had effectively become the US Army Air Force's principal four-engined long-range heavy bomber. Despite its excellent war record, for this reason, the B-17G did not continue long in a frontline role after the cessation of hostilities. Many Eighth and Fifteenth Air Force B-17s were subsequently flown back in stages to the US by their returning crews after the war ended, with a large proportion of these later broken up at huge desert depositories. Some surviving B-17s were converted for photographic reconnaissance and cartographic work, while others were used in various trials or as transports – these were usually low airframe-hours aircraft that went through little, if any, proper action. Sadly, many veterans that had amassed impressive records in air combat, including several that had survived more than 100 missions, were unceremoniously scrapped.

The B-17's role as a transport commenced early in World War Two, and a dedicated variant, the C-108, had been created. For the B-17G, there were two specific conversions – the CB-17G, which was a troop transport, and the VB-17G. The latter was an umbrella term covering various B-17Gs made into staff transports, often with their armament reduced or removed, and well-appointed interiors added. No two conversions were alike, as they were mainly created at theater level, and a number of top-brass used these ad hoc conversions both during the war and afterwards.

Flying Fortresses were used for trials and test work after World War Two. This aircraft, 44-85818, was built as a B-17G-110-VE but was converted postwar in the comparatively extensive radio-controlled drone/controller program. It wears the nose insignia of the 1946 Bikini Atoll atomic bomb test group, which used radio-controlled B-17s to sample the atomic cloud following the two detonations (Operation *Crossroads*) at Bikini Atoll in July 1946. (USAAF)

"Buzz Numbers" were assigned to US military aircraft post-World War Two, with "BA" being used as the prefix for all surviving B-17s. This example, seen with several RAF-marked aircraft including an Avro York, was 42-102803, a B-17G-60-BO. (USAAF)

Rescue Fortresses

As previously mentioned, B-17 production ended with the G-model. All subsequent Flying Fortress versions were therefore conversions of already-existing airframes. Important among these was the B-17H. This B-17G derivative (after 1948, it was redesignated as SB-17G) was a search and rescue (SAR) designation covering a variety of aircraft for several of the US armed services, including airborne lifeboat-carrying. Developed during World War Two, the B-17H was converted initially in small numbers from the B-17G, to carry an air-droppable Higgins A-1 airborne lifeboat mounted beneath the fuselage. Small numbers of these aircraft operated in both northwest Europe and the Pacific theater during the latter stages of World War Two. At that time, these aircraft were armed. Approximately 130 B-17Gs were eventually modified, or intended to be modified, to B-17H standard, although opinions differ as to exactly how many. After the war ended, the defensive armament was removed and a search radar was installed in some examples, where the B-17G's chin turret had previously been fitted. Some served in the Korean War and were armed with flexible-mounted machine guns in several positions, making them the last armed US-operated Flying Fortresses.

During and after World War Two, a number of weapon systems were tested on specially converted B-17s. Included were Ford-Republic JB-2 Loon unguided missiles, which were US reverse-engineered examples of the German V-1 flying bomb. Other Flying Fortresses were employed on various other trials programs. One of these involved testing the AN/APQ-7 radar, later fitted successfully to Boeing B-29 Superfortresses of the 315th BW in precision raids against Japanese targets, in the latter stages of World War Two. By the later 1950s, the final B-17Gs in USAF service were DB-17 drone controllers and unmanned QB-17 drones, together with a dwindling number of VB-17G transports. The last official operational flight made by a USAF Flying Fortress was on August 6, 1959, when DB-17P 44-83684 directed a QB-17 (identified in some sources as 44-83717 or 44-83727) from Holloman Air Force Base (AFB), New Mexico, as a target for a live air-to-air guided missile firing test. A retirement ceremony was held several days later at Holloman AFB, after which 44-83684 was sent for storage at Davis-Monthan AFB – it was subsequently preserved and later flew as *Piccadilly Lilly II* with the Planes

The comparatively small number of VIP VB-17G transports flew a wide range of famous people; 44-83237 was used by USAAF General Carl Spaatz and carried his four stars beneath the starboard cockpit windows. It was called *Boops*, a nickname for his daughter. (USAAF)

A lifeboat-carrying SB-17G of Flight D, 5th Rescue Squadron, USAF. These operational rescue Fortresses carried high-visibility markings, as well as radar equipment in the lower forward fuselage where the chin turret was originally installed. (USAF)

of Fame collection at Chino, California; the aircraft had served during the latter stages of World War Two as *Piccadilly Lilly* with the 447th BG. It seems possible, however, that at least one target drone B-17 was shot down in 1960; apparently, a QB-17L was recorded as destroyed by an IM-99 Bomarc ground-to-air missile.

US Navy service

It is often forgotten that the Flying Fortress proved useful to the US Navy and US Coast Guard following World War Two, but this was of course in a strictly land-based capacity. The basic but roomy B-17 airframe was highly suitable for the installation of the equipment the Navy wished to install, and the type's excellent endurance enabled – as discovered by the RAF's Coastal Command during World War Two – long-range patrol sorties to be flown on a regular basis. Nevertheless, this naval usage was on a comparatively small scale.

With the commencement of the Cadillac II program for land-based long-range Airborne Early Warning, Command and Control by the US Navy, the USAAF allocated 20 brand new Douglas-built B-17Gs, serialed between 44-83855 and 44-83884, forming the nucleus of the US Navy radar-equipped PB-IW program. They received the US Navy Bureau Numbers 77225 to 77244. The aircraft were transferred to the US Navy at Johnsville, Pennsylvania. They had their defensive armament deleted and were fitted with AN/APS-20 search radar in a large "belly" radome beneath the fuselage for maritime search and surveillance duties under the designation PB-1W. More appear to have been obtained but

The US Navy and US Coast Guard used a comparatively small number of Fortresses. This PB-1W, BuNo 77258 (an ex-B-17G), shows the prominent under-fuselage radar bulge of this mark, containing an AN/APS-20 search radar. Most PB-1Ws were unarmed but this example, unusually, retains its guns. (US Navy)

A USAF SB-17G demonstrates the release in flight of its Higgins A-1 airborne lifeboat. This was an impressive sight, and apparently, there was a high percentage of success with such releases, although the concept is not used nowadays. (USAF)

Several converted drone former B-17Gs were used for Operation *Crossroads*, the atomic detonations at Bikini Atoll in the Pacific in July 1946. Each was marked differently, and several are seen here prior to deployment. (USAAF)

presumably were not converted, although one served as an engine testbed. A handful of US Navy squadrons flew the PB-1W, including the development squadron VX-4, Composite Squadron VC-11 at NAAS Miramar in California, and the frontline VW-1. There was a single PB-1, which was a B-17F brought up to roughly B-17G standard for research work, including the carrying of a replica Grumman F8F Bearcat fighter beneath the fuselage for aerodynamic testing.

The US Coast Guard used some 17 B-17Gs (Douglas and Lockheed-Vega built) as the PB-1G, most being converted to B-17H/SB-17G SAR standard with a Higgins A-1 airborne lifeboat beneath the fuselage. All PB-1W and PB-1G US Navy/Coast Guard aircraft operated primarily after World War Two, and the Coast Guard retired the last PB-1G during 1959, making it quite possibly the last US military Flying Fortress in operation.

Some sources quote the US Coast Guard as operating 18 PB-1G Flying Fortresses, all ex-B-17G airframes, as exemplified by this lifeboat-carrying example. The final aircraft, BuNo 77254, was retired officially at Elizabeth City, North Carolina, in October 1959. (US Navy)

This US Navy PB-1W is undergoing engine overhaul and wing repair at Barber's Point Naval Air Station, Oahu, Hawaii, by men of VW-1. Early Navy Fortresses were natural metal, but later received this smart coat of Gloss Sea Blue (which appears to have been the same as that used late in World War Two for US Navy aircraft). (US Navy)

Export machines

In addition to US and British service, Flying Fortresses (particularly B-17Gs) were also used by several foreign military arms. This was almost exclusively after World War Two, and Flying Fortresses also served extensively after the war with civil operators in various parts of the world. At least one was specially fitted for aerial spraying of the pesticide DDT. Some also appeared in films such as *The War Lover* and one of the all-time classic war movies, *Twelve O'Clock High*. Some were also used in the 1989 over-dramatization of the story of the final mission of the famous Eighth Air Force B-17F *"Memphis Belle"* – during the filming of which one priceless airworthy Fortress was destroyed.

A comparatively large number of countries therefore operated the Flying Fortress after World War Two in military service, or in civilian guise under military contract, while in others B-17s appeared on the relevant country's civil register. This employment was almost exclusively for transport, rescue, firebombing or cargo use, and usually consisted of surplus low-hours former US-operated or stored aircraft (no B-17s were ordered as such for new-build manufacture by overseas buyers). Among the countries involved were Argentina, Bolivia, Brazil, Canada, Colombia, Denmark, the Dominican Republic, France, Iran, Israel, Mexico, Nicaragua, Peru, Portugal, South Africa, the Soviet Union, and Sweden. In Brazil and Portugal, lifeboat-equipped Fortresses were operated for SAR operations, the Brazilian SB-17Gs serving principally with the 6th Grupo at Recife. One country in particular – Bolivia – took a liking to the veteran B-17Gs, and its Servicio Aéreo Boliviano (with, for example, CP-891) and Lloyd Aéreo Boliviano became well known for operating the type.

Among foreign military operators, Israel used its Flying Fortresses in combat. Three aircraft appear to have been involved, which were obtained in the US and subsequently prepared in Czechoslovakia for Israeli military service. Makeshift external bomb racks were installed, as well as non-standard gun mountings in the waist and tail positions. Flown mainly by former USAAF personnel, the three B-17s left Žatec in Czechoslovakia on July 15, 1948. They were assigned to 69 "Hammers" Squadron of the Israeli Defense Force/Air Force (IDF/AF).

A considerable number of combat-damaged US bombers made their way to neutral countries during wartime bombing raids. Both Switzerland and Sweden became havens for damaged B-17 and B-24 bombers, which were unable to return to their bases following battle damage, and both countries eventually ended up with various potentially flyable B-17s of different marks. In the case of Sweden, several B-17s were repaired and converted into makeshift airliners. Operated by AB Aerotransport, they are thought to have been the only dedicated B-17 commercial airliners and could carry 14 passengers in their specially modified but narrow fuselages. Seven are known to have worn Swedish civil registrations (as SE-BAH, SE-BAK, SE-BAM–BAP, SE-BAR), three being B-17Fs and the rest B-17Gs. Boeing itself attempted to create a special passenger-carrying conversion of existing B-17s as executive transports under the designation Model 299AB. The plan failed, although the airline TWA did employ a modified B-17G with a well-appointed interior and several airliner-style windows in the fuselage sides.

Trials and mapping

A further use for surplus B-17s was that of trials and testbed aircraft. Three Flying Fortresses were significant testbeds for a new breed of engine, the turboprop. This type of powerplant is commonplace today, but in the later 1940s it was still in its infancy. A trio of B-17s in particular served as important engine testbeds and performed valuable work in the development of new engine concepts. Two were converted by Boeing as the Model 299Z in 1947 and 1948, these being Vega-built B-17G-105-VE 44-85734 and B-17G-110-VE 44-85813, which were then sometimes referred to with an EB-17G designation, later changed to JB-17G. They were modified so that a fifth engine could be mounted in the nose, giving each a very distinctive appearance. Considerable reconstruction work was needed on each aircraft to enable this new configuration, with the flight deck of each moved rearwards for center of gravity considerations, and a large mounting structure added in each forward fuselage to accommodate the new engine configuration. Test instrumentation was installed in a revised crew position in the former fuselage bomb bay. Airframe 44-85734, which joined the US civil register as N5111N, subsequently tested the Pratt & Whitney XT-34 turboprop of some 5,500shp. With

An attempt at creating improved B-17 performance was the XB-38, powered by four Allison V-1710-89 liquid-cooled inline engines, replacing the usual Wright R-1820 radials of production Fortresses. The project showed promise and would have led to an improved B-17G derivative, but the program was cancelled in August 1943. (USAAF)

Based at Creil near Paris, the Institut Géographique National's fleet of converted B-17Gs became a familiar sight not just in France, but in many other parts of the world where their specialist services were required. F-BGSP was originally 44-8846, a B-17G-85-VE, and was later preserved in France as *The Pink Lady*. (Malcolm V Lowe Collection)

this engine operating, the B-17 could quite easily fly with just the turboprop running and the four normal R-1820 radial engines stopped. 44-85813 flight-tested the similarly experimental Wright XT-35 turboprop of 5,000shp under the civil registration N6694C, and was also used in development work on the Wright R-3350 engine – similarly mounted in the nose of the aircraft. A third B-17G, 44-85747, was also converted to five-engine configuration, although with less reconstruction work on its airframe, and tested the Allison T-56 turboprop. Of these aircraft, 44-85734 N5111N survived its conversion (albeit subsequently returned to normal four-engined status) as *Liberty Belle* of The Liberty Foundation in Tulsa, Oklahoma, as N390TH.

A variety of B-17s performed important work as survey aircraft. France's mapping and cartographic agency, the Institut Géographique National (IGN), operated several Fortresses converted for aerial mapping and photography. These were unarmed machines equipped by the French with several specific technical standards for photography, airborne mapping and cartography. The initial aircraft were received from 1947 onwards. Based at Creil in northern France but operating as required in many parts of the world, a nucleus of IGN Fortresses survived well into the 1970s, at a time when considerable interest was being generated in the preservation of historic aircraft. Some of the currently surviving B-17G "warbirds" in private hands are former IGN aircraft, and it is thanks to their long-running service in France that these aircraft still exist today.

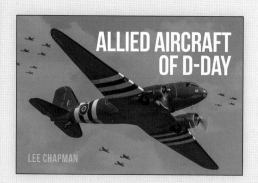
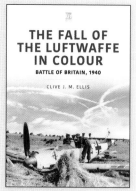
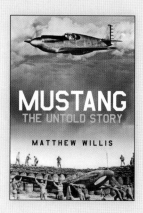
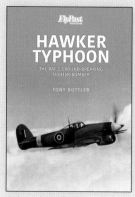
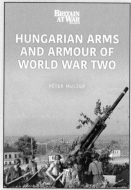